CW01206881

Mi Vida Loca

The Crazy Life
of
Johnny Tapia

©2006 by Johnny Tapia
All rights reserved

Except for appropriate use in critical reviews or works of scholarship, the reproduction or use of this work in any form or by any electronic, mechanical, or other means now known or hereafter invented, including photocopying and recording, and in any information storage and retrieval system is forbidden without the written permission of the publisher.

10 09 08 07 06   1 2 3 4 5

Library of Congress Cataloging-in-Publication Data

Tapia, Johnny, 1967-
  Mi vida loca : the crazy life of Johnny Tapia / Johnny Tapia, with Bettina Gilois.
    p. cm.
  Includes bibliographical references and index.
  ISBN 1-56625-271-7 (alk. paper)
  1. Tapia, Johnny, 1967- 2. Boxers (Sports)--United States--Biography. I. Gilois, Bettina. II. Title.

GV1132.T36A3 2005
796.83'092--dc22

                                    2005024866

Cover and Interior Design: Joy Jacob
Cover Photo: ©Lauren Greenfield/VII310.435.3825

Volt Press
9255 Sunset Blvd., #711
Los Angeles, CA 90069
www.volt-press.com

Mi Vida Loca

The Crazy Life of Johnny Tapia

By Johnny Tapia
and
Bettina Gilois

Volt Press
Los Angeles

To Teresa

My name is Johnny Lee Tapia.
I was born on Friday the 13th.
A Friday in February of 1967.
To this day I don't know if that makes me lucky or unlucky.

When I was eight I saw my mother murdered.
I never knew my father.
He was murdered before I was born.
I was raised as a pit bull.
Raised to fight to the death.

Four times I was declared dead.
Four times they wanted to pull life support.
And many more times I came close to dying.

But I have lived and had it all.
I have been wealthy and lost it all.
I have been famous and infamous.
Five times I was a world champion.

You tell me. Am I lucky or unlucky?

1

MY MOTHER, VIRGINIA, SHE WAS A BEAUTIFUL WOMAN, WITH BEAUTIFUL BLUE EYES. She used to call me her "Little Boy Blue," and I was blue like her blue eyes, blue in those little blue suits she used to dress me in. Little fancy blue suits with shorts and suspenders and the nice trim on them. She'd take me to the photographer and get me my picture taken. You see a skinny little boy, and I was real small, with big dark eyes, dressed in a fancy little suit, smiling real hard.

My mother had nothing but the best for her son. We may have lived in the barrio. We may have been poor. But my mama always dressed me in those little blue suits and she made me feel special. She never let me feel poor.

They used to call my mother "Santa Claus." She was always giving things away. She always had a candy for you, always had a treat. If she came to visit you, she always had a gift. Neighborhood kids smiled when they saw her coming. They would surround her and she'd empty her pockets. Anything she had, to family and strangers, she'd give it all away. Most of all her love. She gave me all her hugs and her kisses. I was a rich boy when I had my mother to give me her love.

But I lost my mother too soon. She was taken from me. Robbed from me. Murdered. Murdered in the worst way you can imagine. Stabbed twenty six times and left for dead.

The night she died I saw her taken away. I was eight years old, pounding on the windowpane, yelling for help, but nobody believed what I saw. There was nothing I could do. And so she died.

And I've been blue ever since. And ever since, I haven't known if I should live or die.

That's the God's honest truth. That's the only way I can say it. As long as my mother's in heaven, there's a calling for me to go.

My mother and I, we lived in a little house on the corner of Lead Avenue and Coal Avenue in Barelas, a neighborhood in Albuquerque, New Mexico.

Barelas is a barrio turf, like many others, where you don't cross the street if you don't know somebody on the other side. Drive down the streets now and you see little houses baking in the sun. Looking at them, you wouldn't know, these streets are dangerous. And they always were.

The house was a small house. Nothing special. Two bedrooms. One bathroom. Little adobe house. Bars on the windows. A little scruff on the ground that was supposed to be the grass.

It's gone now. They tore it down and made a parking lot.

These days I live up on the mountainside so high I can't even see the ghetto. I come down and drive by the old neighborhood and I can still see that house in my mind. I can still see my mother, dancing inside.

The Christmas decorations were always up. We kept them out all year, lighting up the house with bright colors. Red and green like chili peppers.

At night, when I was little, I'd look out the window and see the lights on the roof and I felt good things were coming to me. It was like we had Christmas all the time.

We lived in that house alone for a long time. Or it seemed like a long time. But when you're little, everything is big and everything takes forever.

It was me in that house, my mom and our dog, Whiskey. He was a big Alaskan Husky, and he had some beautiful blue eyes himself.

He'd sleep in my bed every night. He'd curl up at the foot of the bed when we went to sleep, and by the morning he'd be sprawled out all over, hogging up all the room, and me on the floor.

For a while my uncle, Randall, who was my mom's little brother, came to live with us, too. He was just a few years older than me, but he was much bigger. We put another bed in my room, and my mother took in her little brother like he was her own. I called him "Dolph." He called me "Miloo." We played together, fought each other, protected each other every day. Me and Randall, we lived like brothers for a long time.

We're still that close.

My mom spoiled me. I won't lie. I was a spoiled little kid. I had the first of everything. I had the first scooter on the block. The first four-wheeler. The first bicycle. And when Randall was with us, he got it, too. She wanted her son to have the best. There's nothing little Johnny didn't get if he wanted it. How she did it, I still don't know.

Some kid would stop me on the street and say, "Hey, Johnny Tapia. You think you're so cool riding that bike?" And then he'd try to steal it. He'd be four inches taller than me, and years older, too. I may have been small, but I was always a hell of a fighter. I'd pound on him with my fists until I had him writhing on the ground and then I'd ride on. If you got some privilege in the ghetto, you better be prepared to defend it.

My mom, every year she'd take me to the Albuquerque State Fair on the first day it opened. Every September we'd walk over to the fairgrounds up Coal Avenue and Lead, then up Silver and Gold Avenue, up to San Pedro. It wasn't good enough taking the other streets. We never took Lead or Coal. She'd say, "Look Johnny, we're walking on silver, we're walking on gold." And when she said it, I could see the streets shining in front of me, and I was sure we were rich. And I'd hold her hand and I'd look up at her and see her smile shine down on me. Nobody had a more beautiful mother than me.

We'd go do the whole fair up and down. We'd see the pigs and the cows and the chickens, which were my favorites, but she liked the rabbits most of all. I'd ride on ponies, shoot balloons, and get a cotton candy as big as me.

She'd enter me in the Penny Carnival Dance Contest for little kids and I won. I won because I'm a dancing machine. Always have been. Inherited that from her. Never shied away from an audience. I took home a trophy and a prize. A little plastic golden cup mounted on a stand and a little Ninja sword, my prize possession. She was so proud of me, she kissed and hugged me all the way home.

Sometimes we had so much luck we couldn't believe it. Once my mom gave me the money to go and buy a raffle ticket at our church. So we bought a ticket and I won a horse. It was a pony. Me. I won a whole pony.

I always wanted a horse. I love horses. I was "Billy The Kid" one year for the parade in Albuquerque.

So my mom and me took this pony home. But as soon as the pony got to my house it was already out. Finished. Done. It was about eighty years old. It was as big as my yard. Could barely fit. Couldn't move, it was so old. It came from the Garcia's. The Garcia's owned "Garcia's Kitchen," a little neighborhood restaurant. It's still there. We used to go and have tacos and talk to the owner. They loved my mom. They were the ones that had donated the pony to the Church Carnival. I loved that pony and I was so proud. I put the reins on, walked it all the way from 4th street to 7th street and back, pulling on the reins, "Come on, Pony." Must have been quite a sight, me and my pony, walking through the ghetto. Not too many ponies there. My mom took pictures and thought I was so cute, and we thought we were so lucky.

But the pony was so old, one day my mom said, "You gotta give it back, Johnny. It's old and sick. We can't keep it anymore. It's cruel." I said, "Awww, come on, Mom. Come on." She said, "No, you gotta give it back, Johnny." She was right. So I gave it back. But for a while I was the luckiest kid who had a pony, thanks to my mom.

She felt bad for my disappointment, so instead she gave me a Buick Riviera, big old thing, standing in my grandpa's back yard. It was a nice, huge car. She said, "Some day, Johnny, that's your car." I saw myself behind the wheel, driving the through the streets of Albuquerque, moving the wheel back and forth the way they do on TV.

She gave me a lot of dreams. She made me think about all the good things I had coming in the future. She'd say, "You're a special boy, Johnny. Don't forget you're special. You're small now, but you're gonna be big someday. You got something special. You're gonna have a big life, you'll see."

My mother had long, thick black hair and stunning blue eyes. Everywhere she went she turned heads. She loved to dance and she danced all the time. Danced in the kitchen if she was cooking. Danced me around the room when she was happy. Danced alone to music when I was supposed to be sleeping in my bed. I'd sneak to the door and peak out and see her in the living room dancing by herself.

Sometimes she'd go dancing with her friends, and then she'd be gone for days. I'd stay at my grandparents house then, and I'd sleep on the floor on the porch. And sometimes I hardly missed her, hardly noticed a whole weekend go by.

There were always at least twelve, sometimes as much as twenty, cousins and uncles also living in that house. They kept me busy, playing and fighting, playing and fighting, and then fighting some more. There was always a lot of noise in that house. So, I had my fun when she'd go dancing.

Then she'd come back, sometimes after a night or two, and she'd look tired and scoop me up and we'd go home and it was just me and her again.

My mother was such a beautiful woman, there were plenty of men who thought so, too. I didn't always like them coming around, but she didn't have much to do with anybody then. She was too free, too beautiful, she belonged to nobody but me.

But then she met Claudio Gallegos and he moved into our house and into our lives she even married him one day and then I had to call him "Pop." Claudio was a big, hard man with a shaved head. He didn't talk to me much, and I didn't like him very much neither.

He drank a lot of beer and he'd yell. He'd yell for his food. Yell for his beer. Yell for his silence. There's nothing he could say without yelling.

He had a big booming voice.

"Johnny, go get me a beer."

"Johnny, get me my cigarettes."

"Johnny, go change the station." Always bossing me around. I stayed up nights thinking of how I was gonna get rid of him.

He tolerated me, but I hated him. Hated how he took over

the house. Hated his friends. Men. Men who'd come and put their feet on our living room table and yell and laugh. Men with tattoos and missing teeth and hard eyes. Eyes always looking over their shoulders.

I hated how it all took her over. At night, she'd come into my room and put me to bed and she'd sing "Hush Little Baby" to me, and I wouldn't know what a mockingbird was or what anybody wanted with one. She'd tell me not to worry about Claudio. And then he'd start yelling and she then had to go again. I'd hug Whiskey and fall asleep to the sounds in the living room.

Honestly, I don't know why she put up with him. But there are things I will never know about my mother. All I know is, she didn't do nothing wrong. She didn't drink, didn't smoke. Didn't do drugs. She loved to love. She had a big heart and a forgiving nature. It wasn't her fault that he was messed up. It was Claudio. It wasn't her fault, who he was. She didn't make him up, he came to her like that, already made.

One night, I heard the yelling, and it got extra loud. Couldn't anybody sleep with that yelling going on. And I could hear in the voice of my mother that something was wrong. Sounded like somebody slapping somebody.

I guess I was scared. Five years old. But I thought my mom was in trouble. I grabbed my Ninja sword and crept into the living room. Saw him hitting her. That's all I could take. Then I saw red.

I ran over and I stabbed that man with my sword, and didn't think nothing about it. He hurt my mother and all I felt was rage. I wanted to kill that man.

So here's Claudio with me on him, stabbing his leg, his arms, wailing at him with my little sword. He's cursing at me, twirling around, trying to pick me off. Needless to say he about swipes me across the room with a sweep of his big arms, but I got up and kept coming at him. You couldn't stop me when I'm on. And you couldn't hurt my mother. That's all that was in my brain. He might' a killed me, and I wouldn't have even known it, and wouldn't have even cared. You couldn't hurt my mother without dealing with me.

After that he treated me okay. I showed that man all right. And he left me alone and he left her alone, too.

Soon after that the cops came one night and raided the house. We had the sirens and the noise and everything. They broke down the front door in the middle of the night. They came in, guns whipping out, loud voices. Got so loud and chaotic, Whiskey ran away. I'm running outside, calling for Whiskey. My mother's crying in the living room. Claudio's got his arms in handcuffs, being pushed into the squad car outside, and that's the last I saw of neither one.

Never got Whiskey back. Never saw Claudio again. That's how life goes sometimes. You take the good with the bad.

2

TAPIA IS THE ONLY NAME I'VE EVER KNOWN.
Without a father, it was like I was sprung from my mother's womb. Everything came from her. My life. My name. My history.

Tapias are a big family in New Mexico. A name you see everywhere.

When you come from New Mexico it's like you're from nowhere. You're not from America. You're not from Mexico. You might as well be from the moon. Half the time people don't even know where it is.

But we Spanish people from New Mexico, we come from the old line of conquistadors. The conquerors of America. They came through looking for gold and made their mark on this land. Everybody from New Mexico with a Spanish last name comes from a conquistador. And everyone has the blood of the old Spanish fighters in them.

I'm a Tapia all the way and I'm proud to wear that name. It's the name of my grandfather and his fathers before him. It's a name that stands for fighting. And the Tapias are known to be fighters, every single one.

My grandpa, Miguel Tapia, was a boxing champ when he was a young man. He boxed in San Miguel County, up near Las Vegas, New Mexico. He lived in a tiny town called Ribera. He boxed and dreamed of being a world champion before he met my grandmother and started the family and became a man. Boxed before he had to work in the mines and then got the black lung, and had to give it all up.

He stole his thirteen-year-old girl, Ester, right out from her family and made her his bride, put her in a house and gave her twelve kids. She rarely left that house again. Never had a chance to grow up, that woman shunned the world. She was all about her family.

Virginia was her first child. Had her when she was fourteen. Both of them growing up together.

My mother was born the first and the most beloved. She was the apple of my grandpa's eye, the pride of her mother's heart. She helped raise her eleven siblings. She was responsible, and strong, and a fighter. She fought for every inch of life she enjoyed. She was a Tapia all the way.

In my family nobody ever cried. You cried, grandpa would smack up upside the head. You complained, you'd get smacked. You talked back, you came home late, you didn't mind, you were on the phone too long, you made a smart remark, you made a funny face, you had a beating coming your way fast.

And a beating was a real beating, nothing soft about it. Not a nice kind of beating. A slam you up against the wall, box your ears, whack you to the floor, crack your head on the furniture kind of beating.

Grandpa would discipline the boys and Grandma would discipline the girls. And in between Ester took the frying pan to my Grandpa Miguel's head, just in case anybody forgot who was boss.

It was all about discipline. About teaching you who is in charge. About respect. Respecting your elders. Respecting the one who puts food on the table. Respecting the one who puts clothes on your back. Acting straight. Acting right. Having honor. Having pride.

How my mom made it out of the house so happy, I don't know. I guess she knew how to act straight. I guess she was special. She never made them no trouble. Never gave them a reason to mistreat her, and they never made her cry.

The only one crying was me. I'd squawk. I'd yell. I was a loud little runt. I was the smallest of the Tapia kids. The youngest. The rowdiest. I had to yell just to be heard.

Hanging with my cousins and uncles meant there was nineteen more than you, bigger, stronger, tougher. And I had to make some noise just to get attention. I'd be in the middle of a bunch of legs and feet most of the time, and take a jab at somebody's rib just to see if they were real.

And they'd pick me straight up and play dodge ball with my butt. It was funny to hang me upside down. It was funny to pick me up, throw me around, tease me, take away my stuff, pull on my little suits, and make fun of me and my runt size. But I never let it get to me. I just came back at 'em. I just made more noise.

Mi Vida Loca

And it's not like my cousins, and uncles, and even my aunts, weren't people to be reckoned with. Every one had been trained on the punching bag hanging out in back that Grandpa Miguel made himself. A sack filled with rocks and sand. He'd be punching it every day after he went running. Took good care of himself, he did. Then he trained each kid in the house how to hit that bag and be a fighter. So, come Friday and I come over for a weekend, they took their turns punching it out on me for a little extra training.

But that extra little something inside me would be going off and I gave as good as I got. I kicked some shins. I punched some noses. I pulled a lot of hair. Jabbed a few eyeballs. You got me going, you couldn't stop me. No matter how small I was, there wasn't a time they didn't end up wishing that they'd never unleashed that beast in me.

That's cause I had something the others didn't have. I had a power plant inside me. I was lit up all day long like a nuclear reactor. Don't nobody know where that come from. And ain't nobody known how to turn it off. I never stopped going. Running all day long. I couldn't sit down. I couldn't sit still. Couldn't stop fidgeting. Couldn't stop talking. My brain running a mile a minute. I couldn't ever just set down and chill. Not me. I come in the house and it was like a freight train.

Drove my grandparents nuts. I'd spend time with them on the weekend if my mom was gone, and they'd right quick pack me up to the Wells Park Community Center and send me right down the street for the whole day.

"Johnny, go play at Wells Park. Don't come home 'til it's dark."

They had programs for kids, street kids, kids like me, with lots of stuff to do, basketball, baseball, trampoline, foosball, gymnastics. All kind of games. I'd be there all day and never sit down, running and running.

I'd jump on that trampoline until they had to throw me off. I did gymnastics 'cause I loved to do flips in the air. I'd stand on the side of the basketball court, crying, 'cause the big kids wouldn't let me play. I was a freak for basketball most of all. That's my first love. The sport I love the most. And after that I loved every single sport and activity you put in my way. I was an athlete, always all the way around. Loved to move. And when it was dark outside, you had to drag me back to the house.

One day, Wells Park put up a flyer, nailed it on a bulletin board, talking about a day trip to Los Alamos. It was at a time when my mom was busy, and my grandparents signed me right up. Sending me off for a whole day was music to them.

We all lined up early in the morning. Me with empty pockets and an empty stomach. We all drew straws and then people's names got called out, assigned to several buses. I got called to the nice new bus, and I was kidding everybody about how I lucky I was, and how I got on the good bus and they got the bad one.

We all got on and that bus took off and drove up the interstate toward Santa Fe and I swear I never saw a more beautiful country. I had never left the ghetto before. It was a huge deal for me. Might as well have sent me to Mars. I looked forward to it for weeks. Couldn't sleep. Couldn't wait.

I sat right in front 'cause I was the first one to get on the bus and the youngest one, too. Sat next to a nice woman with a big belly, a baby on the way. Her name was Concha. She had a sweet face and she was so nice to me. She gave me candy and treats and talked to me the whole way on the drive. Or maybe I talked to her. I probably never stopped talking. But she smiled the whole way and laughed at all my jokes.

We got to Los Alamos and walked in the mountains. Hiking. The only hike I ever took was when my grandpa told me to get outta his sight when I was being too loud. I'd hike my butt out of that room real quick.

Now here we were walking in the forest. I still remember the sound of the dry sticks and leaves under my feet. I still remember the smell of pine. Didn't smell nothing like the Pine-Sol my grandma scrubbed down the house with every day.

I was seven years old. Thought it was all pretty damned amazing. Never saw the earth spread out so wide like from that mountain top. Never had seen how far things can go beyond the street grid of the ghetto. Never realized until then, just how big the world really was.

And on the way back, I felt real big myself. I swear I felt like I had grown three inches. Couldn't wait to get home and try out my new size on my cousins.

We were all happy on that bus. Everybody singing songs.

Everybody made friends. Concha making sure I ate. I sat in my seat and we shared our chips and soda and candy. The bus driver's waving his big paper bag of candy for anyone to take.

It's getting late and that bus is going down and down that mountainside, winding down, everybody swaying left to right, rocking with the curves.

Suddenly we catch a rock. The bus jumps and groans. The bus driver hits the brakes, but the brakes lock, don't catch, don't stop.

So we skid. People are screaming now.

The driver yells. "Keep it quiet! Keep it quiet!"

People keep screaming.

The bus hits a railing. And now we flip over, flip right off the side of that mountainside. Eighty feet down we fell in that bus.

People are bellowing. People are flying through the air. People hitting the ceiling, knocking into each other, food and drinks are flying over everything. And for a moment it feels like we're never gonna stop.

Then the worst thing happens. It is a vision I will never forget. The bus finally hits and catches the side of the mountain, slides down the hillside and doesn't stop until we hit a tree.

I get thrown down the front of the bus and the pole by the door catches me. Catches me hard. Gives me a concussion. Cracks my head right open.

That same second, I see Concha. She flies right past me. Flies right through the front window. Hits that tree before the

Mi Vida Loca

bus does.

And then the bus hits her.

I saw a woman die, a pregnant woman die, right before my seven-year-old eyes. It should've been me dying right along with her. It was the pole that saved my life.

That's just what I'm telling you. I don't know, if I'm the luckiest, or the unluckiest person come on this world.

Ambulances came to take us to Santa Fe Hospital. I was so scared. All alone. Never been in an ambulance before. Never been in a hospital. The whole thing was on the news. Later it would turn out the bus driver had more than just candy in those paper bags he was waving. He had been drinking. It was a real tragedy. The nurses were all over us, making a big fuss.

But as much as I was in pain, and my head was bandaged, and my bones all hurt, it wasn't nothing compared to a bigger hurt that came in the hours after we got to that hospital.

Pretty soon, the beds all spread out in the hallways and packed into the rooms, pretty soon, the families all start coming in. All the loved ones, all the fathers and mothers and brothers and sisters.

"Honey, I was so worried."

"Oh my God, baby, you're alive!"

"Hito, hito, you scared me to death!"

Mothers sobbing, holding their babies, fathers holding back, flexing their jaws, hiding their tears.

But nobody came for me. Alone overnight, I was scared to death. Every time that door would open, my heart would jump and I'd be sure there was somebody coming for me.

But they never did. The nurses just patched me up. The governor sent a plane, and they sent me back home on that plane the next day, all by myself, scared.

Why didn't nobody come? Why didn't anybody come for me? Where was my mom?

I don't like to think about it still. I don't know why she didn't come. I don't even know if anybody ever told her.

I guess I knew then my family wasn't the normal kind of family you could have. I saw all those people and they looked different. They looked like something held them together that I didn't know that well. That rushing-to-your-side kind of caring about each other. That protective kind of love, that kind of worry that takes you in its arms and holds you tight.

If she had really known, she would have been there. I believe that in my heart. My mother was always the only one to touch me with that kind of love.

But I was alone that time. Hurt me more than my head. Hurt me more than anything else I ever remember.

3

ON THE DAY SHE WAS MURDERED, MY MOTHER TELLS ME SHE IS GOING TO TAKE ME TO MY GRANDPARENTS' HOUSE SO THAT SHE CAN GO OUT DANCING. It was Saturday, May 24th, 1975. I was eight years old. I didn't want her to go that day. I had a strong feeling that she shouldn't go. I still don't know why.

Those days we were living with my Auntie Helen. She had a son herself, a job, a car, and room for us both. When Claudio went to jail, we couldn't make it on our own anymore. Don't ask me how we ever did. I don't remember my mother ever working.

Every weekend my mother went out to dance those days. To the "Far West" dancehall or the "Cow Palace." Spanish dancing. Ranchera music. Al Hurricane. Roberto Griego, Tiny Morrie. She met her friends there and had a good time.

Every weekend I stayed with my grandparents and loved the chaos of all my cousins and the basketball games at Wells Park.

But this day was different. I didn't want her to go. I started whining before we got in the car.

Auntie Helen had a yellow Pinto and we piled in that day and I'm whining and not wanting to go. My mom, always patient, always cheerful, just turns on the radio and sings to Freddy Fender "Before the Next Teardrop Falls" as we drive to my grandparents' house. Me, I'm playing with the window crank, pouting, looking outside. Trying not to look at her. Trying to punish her. Trying not to see that smile of hers, break my concentration.

Helen had her life together pretty good. She was the only sister who really did. Two other sisters, Crucita, Vicky, were in and out of jail so much for drugs, their six kids each lived almost full time with my grandparents.

Helen worked in the accounting department of the university. Her son, Steven, was a nerdy, sensitive kid with glasses and he never got in trouble, even though he wanted to. But Helen kept a tight grip on him, wouldn't let him go bad.

She sure didn't like me staying over at the house too much. I was too wild for her. Always boxing Steven in the head. And me and Steven always got into it all the time. Half the time I was beating him up. The other half I had to beat up others to protect him 'cause he got picked on so much. We were always back and forth like that, me and Steven.

So Helen was glad to get me out of her hair for the weekend and let my mom borrow the car.

"Go have fun, Virginia. I don't need the car 'til work on Monday."

"Thank you, Elena. I'll be back before you need to go to work."

"Be careful," Helen would say.

"I'm careful, don't worry, I always am," my mother always answered.

Every Hispanic family in New Mexico ends their conversations with, "Be careful." You go to work, to the grocery store. You go to the movies. You drive home. They send you off with, "Be careful."

Like you need to go to be on guard all the time.

Like things can go bad. And they can.

My grandpa stands in the door, jingling the change in his pockets, like he always did. My mom went up to him and kisses him on the cheek.

"Hello, Papacito."

"Hello, hita."

He has a hard, weathered face from all those years in the mines and after that, twenty-five years as a custodian for the city. Work that makes your face turn to stone.

But there's a special look in his eyes whenever he sees her. It's a pride thing. It's a love thing. He'd never say it, but it's in his face. She was his first. She is the special one. The beautiful one.

I walk by him and he throws me some punches like he always does. This time I don't punch back. Just walk on, mad. Go inside and don't wanna play with anybody.

My mother's in the kitchen now, fixing her makeup in the mirror, ironing her clothes for the evening. A white ruffled shirt. Some blue slacks.

She looks tired and sees it in the mirror. Touches her eyes.

Lisa, her little sister, watches her fascinated. My mom gives her the scarf around her hair. Gives it to her as a present just because she likes it. There was nothing she wouldn't give away just to make you happy.

My grandma is feeding the kids. Like all these Hispanic families, my grandma was a mom at the same time as her daughters were. Her oldest was thirty two and her youngest was eleven. She's got a baby in her arm taking the bottle, got another one hanging on her apron, got ten kids at the table eating tortillas and beans. She's tied a rope around them just to keep them in their seats and eating.

My mother is saying, "I'm tired. I don't know if I should go out tonight."

Ester says, "Then why go. Stay home."

"I don't know. I promised Richard to go dancing."

"I don't like that Richard, hita. Why do you go out with him? There's something not right about him."

"It's not serious with Richard, Mama. I just like someone to go dance with."

"Don't let him make you trouble, hita. Like Claudio did."

"I won't let him, Mama. I'm done with trouble."

"Still you look tired. Why don't you just stay home?"

She keeps ironing, not feeling right.

"It's okay. I said I'd go. I'll have fun."

And even though she doesn't want to, she goes anyway.

When she's walking to the car, I'm pulling on her sleeves and crying.

"Don't go. Don't go out tonight. Mama, don't go out."

But she keeps me off like a little fly.

"Johnny, stop that."

"Don't go out, Mama. Stay here. I don't want you to go, Mama. Please don't go."

She's trying to walk.

"I'll be back soon, Johnny. Let go of me, Johnny. What's wrong with you? This isn't like you."

"I just don't want you to go! Mama, please!"

She stops and kneels down to face me and takes my face in her hands.

"It's okay, Johnny. I'll be back soon."

I'm not looking at her, holding on to her hands. I am fingering her ring. The ring with the yellow stones. I fiddle with her red coral necklace, I touch her long black hair, blubbering, my eyes down.

"Please, Mom, I don't want you to go."

She opens her purse and she gives me a Snickers bar. Strokes my hair.

"I know. Here, Johnny. Look what I got for you."

I always loved candy. I take it and pout.

"I love you, baby. I'll be back soon. And we'll go home, okay?"

Then she gets in the Pinto. I'm sniffling, eating the Snickers bar, watching her drive off.

That night I couldn't sleep. The whole house was sleeping and I was awake. My grandparents are in their bedroom. My fifteen cousins and uncles are sleeping in their places on the floor, half of them without even a blanket. This is how they

33

slept every night.

I was in the little porch at the front of the house, lying on the floor by myself, staring at the ceiling, getting up pacing the room, looking out for her car.

Finally I lie down, feeling drowsy when headlights light up the room. I hear a car outside. I get up and go to the window.

I look outside and there's a blue and green pick up truck, driving by real, real slow. In the back of the truck I see my mother. She's chained to the truck and she's screaming for help.

I start banging on the windowpane.

"Mom! Mom!"

In the cab of the truck, I can't see their faces. But there are two men, I see their silhouettes. They look like they're looking straight at me.

My mom is screaming, and I'm screaming and crying, calling her name, "Mom, Mom, Mom!" But she can't hear me.

And then the truck drives off.

I run into my grandparent's bedroom. I am shaking my grandpa, "Wake up, wake up! You gotta get up! They got my mom! Some men got my mom!"

Grandpa Miguel tries to make me stop shouting. I'm crying, shaking him. I won't listen. I won't stop. He shoves me across the room.

"Shut up, Johnny! Go back to sleep. You had a dream. You had a bad dream."

I keep crying. He's gotta push me away several times.

"Go back to bed, Johnny. It's just a dream."

I finally give up. I don't have a choice. I'm just a kid. A kid has no power. A kid doesn't know anything. I'm not sure what's true anymore.

Did I just have a dream?

The next morning, my mother's not home. It wasn't unusual, but I don't feel right. Everybody's eating breakfast. Everybody's acting like nothing's wrong. But I can't eat. Nothing feels right.

"Where's Mom?"

"She'll be here, Johnny."

I stand on the side of the road, watching for any car, for any sign of my mother.

A car drives up and a man looks outside. This was Richard. He looks at me.

"Hey, Johnny. You wanna come buy some shoes? Your mom wants me to buy you some shoes. Come and get in the car."

Ester comes out behind me and stops me.

"What do you want, Richard?"

"I'm supposed to pick Johnny up to buy shoes."

She says, "No. Johnny stays here."

He asks her, "Is Virginia here? She's got my wallet. I lost my wallet last night and I think she's got my wallet."

My grandma rarely stepped into the sunlight, never left the inside of her house. She's standing there, looking at him a long moment, her copper color hair looking like its on fire in that sun.

"I don't know anything about that."

"That wallet had my pay check in it. Two weeks pay. I need that money"

"I thought Virginia was with you."

"I went home early. She wanted to stay," he says.

"Well, she's not here now."

Then he gets angry.

"Well, you better tell her I'm looking for her. You better tell her to call me. I want my wallet."

Then he guns the car and drives off and is gone.

Nobody thought it was strange for him to come by without her. The day goes by. It's like nobody wants to think anything bad. I keep watching the faces of my grandparents, watch their expressions, to see if I can see anything wrong. Nobody wants to talk to me.

Then it's Sunday and Helen is over and my mom is still not back. Helen is getting worried about her car.

"Why wouldn't she be back by now? She knows I need that car."

"I'm sure she'll be here." Ester is still trying to sound calm, but it's getting harder.

"It's been two days, Mama."

"She can take of herself. It's not the first time."

"How could she leave me without a car?"

"She'll come soon. She always does."

"It's been three days."

By now I feel so sick, I can't eat. I don't understand why everybody's acting all normal.

"Where's mom? When's she coming home?"

Nobody answers me.

"There's something wrong, Grandma. I know it."

Nobody's calling police. They don't even think to call police. When you live in the ghetto the last thing you do is call the police. The police are the enemy. The police stand for everything bad. You don't call police.

I feel so sick now I don't eat at all. Don't want to do anything. Just stand by the window, waiting.

I try to say a couple of times, "Where's my mom at?" Nobody wants to talk to me.

Monday morning. Helen's over and she's mad. Grandpa drives her to work in his old, yellow pick up truck. He comes home with the newspaper and they both go white when they look at it.

There's a story in it. "Woman Found Stabbed In South Albuquerque Area." There's a picture of her jewelry. The ring with the yellow stones. The red coral necklace. No one knows her name. She's in the hospital in a coma.

I watch helpless as Grandpa Miguel's face looks hard and ashen and he gets his keys.

"What's wrong? Where's my mom?"

Ester is pale and gathers her purse. Helen follows. They go out to the yellow truck.

"I wanna go with you!"

I run after them and I am begging them.

"Take me with you. I wanna see my mom! I wanna see my mom!"

I want to see her. I want to be with her. I need to see her

so bad. I'm crying and crying. But nobody wants to deal with a screaming kid. They tell me real strict, "You stay home."

Then they drive off. I think I cried for the rest of the day. I think I cried for the whole night. I didn't eat, I didn't sleep any more. I begged to see her all the time and all I got was "no." I wanted to see her so bad but all I got was "no."

But everyone was in shock. Nobody could handle me. The police were asking questions. No one knew if she was gonna make it. No one knew who did this to her. They had no time to deal with me. My mom was dying. They stayed at the hospital, watching her, waiting. Hoping.

And then she was gone.

My grandpa comes inside the porch with Ester late that night and looks at me hard. He says, "Johnny. I gotta talk to you." I sit down. Scared.

"Your mother's dead. She won't be coming back no more. Never again, Johnny."

I start crying as quickly as I can take a breath.

"No, you're lying. It's not true!"

Grandpa hits me across the face, hits me so hard I fall back on the floor. He's hovering over me, shaking. Shaking with grief and rage.

"Don't cry, Johnny. You don't cry no more. Your mother's gone and there's nothing will change that. Now you can't cry no more. A man doesn't cry. A man doesn't show his feelings."

And that's how they leave me alone. I am sitting in the corner, shaking with my sobbing. And I know they meant to do right. And I know they were filled with pain, and just didn't know what to do with a little kid who was gonna make a lot of noise. But something died in me with my mother that day. Something in my heart was never the same.

I felt so helpless. No one had heard me. No one had listened. Could I have saved her? These thoughts are in my head over and over again, and I am alone.

The rosary. The viewing. The burial. I was kept from it all. I pleaded and begged. But they kept me at home.

I never got to say good-bye to my mom. It's a hurt I have not overcome. It has left such a hole inside my heart. She was taken so violently, I wanted to see her so bad, but they kept me away. And I never got to say good-bye to my mother.

And I could never close that hole in my heart after that.

4

FROM ONE DAY TO THE NEXT, MY LIFE WAS GONE.

I lived at my grandparents' house full time. I got my permanent spot sleeping on the floor in the porch, still sleeping alone. I slept when I could. Most nights I was awake and pacing the house. I paced like a caged animal, watching everybody else sleeping.

I kept hearing noises, kept thinking she might be at the door, coming home. It was worst when I slept. When I slept I dreamt, and I always dreamt my mother was back, and she's there with me and she's so real, and I'm back home with her and she's got her arms around me, and then I woke up and realized she's gone and dead. And it was like losing her all over again. I felt so lonely and empty inside, that I'd rather not sleep at all.

My grandparents' house was filled with religious images, religious figures, statues, pictures, trinkets. My grandparents never went to Sunday church, but the house is filled with the religious like they were the holiest people on this earth. On the table and cupboards there were candles and figures of Mary and Jesus, and the Guadalupe Virgin, and St. Anthony,

St. Francis. They're covered in plastic roses, in rosaries. Every night when I walked through the house, I touched the faces of the Virgin, touching their folded hands and thinking of my mother's hands, touching their mouths and remembering my mother's kisses, touching their robes, wishing I had my mother back with me.

But if I thought of her in my heart, I never said a word to the outside. My grandparents didn't want to hear about her from me. After the funeral and the condolences were past, nobody ever mentioned her again. It was like she became erased. Nobody wanted to touch that pain. So I kept her all to myself. And I bore my pain alone.

I lined up with the rest of the kids like everything was normal and held out my hands, waiting for my piece of white bread with mustard for breakfast.

First time I look down at my bread and ask where the real breakfast was, and my grandpa knocks me upside the head.

"You be grateful for what you get. You respect those that put food on the table."

I never asked again. I ate bread and mustard like it was the best thing I ever seen.

On bad days, which was most days, there's bread and mustard. On a good day we all got some Dr. Pepper in a cup. Grandma Ester would get a key from her hiding place in the bedroom and unlock the pantry in the kitchen and bring out the food. Then she'd portion it out, for every kid a little bit. She kept the food locked up all the time. There wasn't nothing you could eat without asking for permission or somebody getting a key.

Dinnertime came chili and beans and potatoes. Every night. Sometimes green chili, sometimes red chili. Chili was always on the stove. Good New Mexican family. Babies were weaned on chili. Everybody eats chili.

I came to live for food. Live for a taste of Dr. Pepper or a candy bar. The only thing that could soften my grief was something sweet. I craved it. I craved those Snickers bars so bad. Like I could get that moment she left back again. It was how I yearned for her. The sweet things calmed me down.

In school I let out all my feelings. Nobody can handle me. I'm a total mess. I never sit, cry, yell, fight with people, I can barely make it through a day. I'm angry. I'm picking fights. I don't listen to nobody. I'm all darkness and rage in an eight-year-old body. I can't see what's happening to me. I see red. I see black. I see darkness and all I know is to push it out of me. And school was the only safe place.

My teachers knew what happened and felt sorry for me. They tried to talk to me, but I'm not for talking. They tried to be patient, but I try their patience over and over again. I made my favorite teacher cry. They sent me to the principal's office, or to the nurse's office, or to the counselor's office. They tried. They really tried to do something with me. They really tried to help. But there wasn't much anybody could do for me then. They were all helpless. As helpless as me. You could see it in their faces. They got this look of pity and fear of me. But I didn't care about them. I didn't care about anything any more.

There wasn't a day of peace since my mother was gone. I

was eight and there was no one looking out for me. I felt all alone. And I knew I had to do what I could for myself.

I came to expect the worst. I was so hyper aware of trouble, they called me "security guard." I would pace at night and listen to the sounds of the ghetto. If there was a gunshot, I'd be the only one to hear it. If there was a strange noise, nobody would notice but me. If someone was hiding in the shadows I'd see them. I was up half the night, listening for the bad things. By three or four in the morning I'd finally fall asleep. And I'm still that way today.

But life had changed and I had to survive. Life became a string of bad things and hard lessons. All the rules had changed. It was like I had to learn how to live all over again. And I learned some real hard lessons.

Me and the other youngest kids are in the house alone one night when I hear a noise. I'm the only one who hears it. I go to the back of the house and see a man climbing in through the window. He's got a masked hat on his head. I see a knife. I start yelling and hollering and waving my arms and running outside. All the other kids run into the street, following me. Nobody's there to help. I go to a neighbor and I'm yelling, "Call the police! Call the police! There's a man in our house!"

They call the police. Police come. Grandparents come home. Here's the black and whites with their lights flashing outside the house, cops waiting to talk to them.

I see my grandpa walking up, his jaw flexing real hard. I'm pretty proud of myself. I'm thinking somebody's gonna pat me on the back this time. Cops take a report and leave. And I get the biggest beating of my life that night because, if you live in the barrio, you don't call the cops.

There's still only one enemy and it's the law. You can be dying, your mother can be dying, your mother can be missing for days. Your mother, who's always been there for you, who's got a heart of gold, who doesn't drink or smoke, who's responsible and loving, doesn't come home for three days and you just don't call the cops. I should have learned it already. It's the rule of the ghetto. You protect your turf. And you never call the cops.

I was a handful. After school was out that summer, my grandparents made me stay out long days and not come home until dark. So, I was out by myself all the time. And some neighbor sees me alone day after day, starts to talking to me, makes jokes, gives me candy. I come to know him.

"Hello, Mr. Julio."

"Hello, Johnny."

"How's your day, Mr. Julio?"

"Good. How you doin', Johnny?"

Then one day, he grabs me from the street and pulls me in his house and puts me in his closet for three days. Burns me with coffee and cigarettes until I wait until he's asleep real good and run away back home. Nobody called the police. Figured I'd come home eventually. I know they didn't know what happened to me. I know they didn't expect that I was locked in a closet. But there were too many kids to think of them all. It was like the boy who cried wolf. I made so much noise, when I was gone they liked the silence too much.

Sitting in that closet, I don't even know what I felt anymore. The world just looked crazy to me. There was nothing to count on. You are always alone. I knew it so deeply for a little kid. You are always really alone.

I never got sick. Or I learned never to get sick. I had survived pneumonia when I was a little kid, nursed and cared for by my mother with love and touch and honey and tea. But my grandparents saw all that differently. Fifteen kids were too many. They never took anyone to the doctor. There wasn't money. There wasn't time. If you were sick, you had to go to school anyway.

When I bit down on a razor blade in a piece of candy, the first Halloween after my mom died, they just made me pull it out myself and left it alone.

When I opened a huge gash in my head, splitting my skull on the trampoline at Wells Park, they made me clean myself up and go home. No stitches.

If anybody had a toothache, my grandpa would come and numb their mouth up with whiskey and lean over with his big frame and pull the tooth right out with pliers. Then he would dig out what was left with a knife.

You better believe I brushed my teeth every day after I lost a couple of teeth that way.

I learned other things, too. It got drummed into me real good. They taught me these things to bring me along, I know it. To help me. To educate me. Motivate me. And I learned it all real good. Like I was the best student.

"There's something wrong with you, Johnny."

"You're no good, Johnny. Never were no good."

"You're never gonna be anything, Johnny."

"You're stupid, Johnny. Do you know that?"

"You're nothing, Johnny."

"You're going nowhere in life, Johnny."

All those words. They came raining down on me.

My old life was gone forever. But the sun still rose every day. The birds still sang outside every morning. A Snickers bar still tasted like heaven. And this new life became the only life I knew. This new life had a lot of pain in it. And I learned that pain is a part of life. And that love can come and go. This was my new life. The life without my mother.

5

FIFTEEN AUNTS AND UNCLES AND COUSINS. They become my new brothers and sisters. And I still call them that today. They become my whole world, and it was a tough world, much tougher at home than the world outside.

All my grandparents' kids still lived at home, other than Auntie Helen. Uncle Randall, or "Dolph," I still called him that, was back with me, back with his own brothers and sisters. Now he's rougher on me 'cause he's got something to prove to everybody else.

Auntie Lisa's there.

Uncle Richard, the oldest son, after my mother. He was such a serious heroin addict, he was always high, always drooling on the couch.

Uncle Oliver who we called "Big-O" was there. He was a rough dude, rough on everybody, especially me.

Uncle Anthony was my grandma's baby, and she loved him so much. We called him "Flox" 'cause he was always so skinny.

Auntie Crucita and Auntie Vicky were both in prison for heroin. So their ten kids lived with my grandparents, too.

Crucita had seven kids.

My cousin, Berna, was the oldest, and real quiet.

There was my cousin Charlie. Charlie had a sweet temper, never really hurt anybody. Unless we called him "Chaleco," which we all did just to make him mad. He was always blow drying his hair. Him and Alfred. We called them both "fasettos" for that. But Charlie was a good guy.

My cousin Raymond, who we all called "Bones," was in the middle. He was the most responsible one and the most troubled one. He's super smart, but damaged from trying to be responsible for all his brothers and sisters while his parents were constantly in jail or high on heroin. He would do anything for his brothers and sisters. Good or bad.

There was cousin Benjamin, who was "Bennie." Bennie was always getting into trouble. Like he was always mad. He stuck to the youngest cousin, little Frankie. Frankie was the baby, and spoiled rotten with a temper to match.

Auntie Vicky had five kids in the house, too.

There was cousin Alfred who we called "911" for a fake suicide attempt he once did.

There was cousin Wilbur, who we called "Fluffy" maybe because even "Fluffy" is better than "Wilbur."

There was cousin Ramona. She stuck with the girls.

There was cousin Joseph, who was kinda quiet.

And there was another daughter, Crystal, but she didn't live there either. She had been given to somebody else to raise. I never knew her, never knew where she lived.

With me that made sixteen kids in a little house with one

bedroom and one bathroom.

Those mouths are a lot of mouths to feed, and my grandpa Miguel went out every day, dressed in his blue custodian's uniform and he worked hard at an honest day's work.

My grandma Ester, she was on her knees everyday, scrubbing the house 'til the floorboards were bleached to white. She was always cooking and cleaning and washing and ironing. She kept the cleanest house in the ghetto, I'm sure of that.

Grandpa Miguel would come home late every night and sit in the kitchen drink his whiskey and Ester would serve him his food, and all he'd ask for is a little respect.

He was a proud man. A man of principles. A man who ruled his own life and everyone else in it.

He loved to say things over and over, his own phrases. "Esta es mi tierra." "This is my dirt." He said it almost every day. He would stomp his foot, usually after drinking his whiskey and getting tired of all us kids making so much noise.

He would tell us all to mind him, and if we still kept talking or screaming or laughing, he'd yell at us to shut up, "Callate!" He would thump his fist on the table. "Esta es mi tierra! You do as I say!"

When he was really drunk he'd start talking about his life, and he'd get all dark and frowning, and start saying how he was a fighter once and how he had to give it all up. How the black lung took his chances away to ever fight again. How his life was spent for work, all for others, and how we all had to be grateful. How he had nobody to thank for what he had. He

Mi Vida Loca

had earned it all himself. He never took a handout. He always worked and always provided for his family. He was fiercely proud of his role as a man and father.

"Yo soy el hombre de mi vida!" he would shout.

"I am the master of my life!"

He demanded respect at all times. He made sure we knew who was boss. And when he was fed up with his ungrateful, disrespectful house full of screaming children, he took away all our privileges, including dinner.

"Yo pago la renta!"

"I pay the rent! You do as I say!"

And he did pay the rent. Sixteen kids lived off of his hard labor. He never let us down. He provided for everybody. I always admired that strength in him. I still do.

When he had had his whiskey and his chili, he'd sit down to watch the Lawrence Welk Show with Ester. It was their favorite show. Or one of the Mexican Variety shows. With ladies in their crazy clothes, and the men in suits and slick hair and moustaches, laughing, rattling off in Spanish, and the Mariachis always ending with a song. My grandparents would sit and watch and chuckle and sometimes even howl with laughter.

Sometimes, I'd lie on the floor in the porch and pretend like I was sleeping and hear the music from the television and hear my grandparents laughing together, and I felt okay then.

Except that my stomach was always empty and it would be growling when I heard him eating his late supper, and I'd have to cover it with my hands, so nobody would hear me be awake and hungry.

Seems like I was always hungry those days. Grandpa would look at me sometimes, jingle his change in his pockets and drop me some quarters in my hand, and I'd run right down the alley behind the house to the "Allsup's" convenicnce store on the corner, and I'd me get me some candy bars.

I'd run down that alley only in the daytime. At night it was much too scary, filled with drug dealers and drunks and perverts and people flashing knives at you. And when you're eight, that shit scares you. It did me. I hated that alley.

Cousin Raymond, Bones, Crucita's oldest son, once came up with a big plan.

Crucita was doing time for a long, long time, and he and his siblings had lived with my grandparents for years. But Raymond always felt like it was still his job to watch out for them. Like a father. He was only fifteen. He had a lot of heart, smart in school. I think he could've been good if the pressure of his life and taking care of his five little brothers and sisters didn't always drive him to being bad.

He was always stealing candy at the Allsup's. He would steal from school. Steal from the grocery store, from the gas station, from somebody's locker. But it was always for his brothers and sisters. Always to buy food, or to get them something they needed, like a pair of shoes. It was never for himself. Except this one time.

So Raymond had the great plan. He said he and I would sneak into the grandparents' room and steal that key to the pantry and go and open it up and help ourselves to all the food and eat until we were full.

So one night, he's awake and he finds me since I'm still awake and pacing around, and he grabs me and puts me up to going in my grandpa's bedroom, the key hanging on a hook right above their heads on the wall.

I have to lean over my sleeping grandma to get the key. I don't breathe. She moans in her sleep and turns and I nearly bolt out of there, but Raymond's at the door, waving at me hard to go and get it.

So one more time I try it, and I got the key and we run to the kitchen and keep our laughing down, Raymond making funny snorting noises with his nose.

He opens the pantry and I swear we saw heaven.

There were rows of Cokes and candy, and jerky meat and cured bacon for Sunday. Crackers and chips, bread and honey, and tortillas and lard and bags of pinto beans.

We grabbed as much as our shirts could hold. Raymond first. He runs off and disappears behind the shed outside. Me, I'm small so I'm having a hard time stuffing it all in my shirt, when I turn and run right into my Grandma Ester.

I never seen a look of fury greater than the fury I saw in her face that night. I look up at her, 'cause even at five foot two she towers above me, and I'm shaking now.

"Grandma," I yell at her, "I'm hungry!"

She doesn't say anything for a long time, just looking down at me like her eyes could laser me into the ground and just leave a little dust spot for her to sweep away.

Well, finally she talks.

"You're no good, Johnny. Always gotta 'cause trouble. Always gotta do something bad. There's something wrong with you, Johnny."

"I'm hungry, Grandma!"

"Don't you respect the memory of your mother? What kinda boy are you? Are you stupid?"

"I'm just hungry, Grandma. That's all."

"You wait until your grandpa hears about this. You got something comin', hito. You got no respect."

Next day, you better believe I got a thrashing of my life. Banging my head against the wall kind of thrashing. Taking out the belt kind of thrashing. There was no mercy. There was only doing what's right. And I had done wrong.

My grandparents never knew about Raymond. And I never told him. That was the rule of the ghetto. You never rat on a partner. I took the beating for both of us, and me and Raymond shared a Snickers bar behind the shed the next day.

Beatings. That's all there was sometimes. That's how it went. I got constant beatings. Half the beatings I took were for somebody else. There were lots of beatings on everybody, but especially on me. So many beatings I got used to them. And it wasn't just my grandpa. He beat me for breaking the rules. But there were also my uncles and my cousins. And they just beat me for fun.

I was the runt of the litter, the smallest of all the Tapia kids, and there's something about picking on the weakest one that some people can't resist. I drew those beatings like a magnet and they just made me stronger. And sometimes, to be truthful, it was the only way I didn't feel the pain. The pain of being alone. The pain of being without my mother.

On weekends I'd get a kick in the ribs by my uncle Oliver, often in the middle of the night when I'm sleeping on the porch, and he'd kick me and tell me to go get him chips and candy from the Allsup's for his munchies. I'd have to take the dollar bills he handed me and run down that alleyway at night. And now I was piss scared. I was so scared of that alley. All the freaks were out there. You'd hear gunshots and see shadows everywhere. Drunks would grin and chase me. The same pervert in the same phone booth would flash me every time I ran by.

By the time I'd ran inside the store, I'm shaking. It's midnight and I'm buying chips and candy and cigarettes for my uncle, Oliver. And I then I gotta run home with them again.

Later he'd be hungry and I'd have to go back for a box of doughnuts.

And I'd go back again. I went because if I didn't go, I'd get the beating of my life. My grandpa was a gentle man compared to what my uncles did to me. And you've gotta know, I love my family. I love every member of my family. With all my heart. They did what they thought was right, they did what they knew, and sometimes right was wrong, and sometimes they didn't know any better. But no matter what they did to me then, they made me what I am today, and today what I am is strong.

That was my life then. And I knew nothing else anymore. I knew you could have a mother who hugged and kissed and loved you and protected you. And I knew that from one minute to the next she could be taken away, and all you are left with is pain and trouble. And you're all alone in the world, and there's nobody there for you, and the pain, that pain becomes what is normal. And when all you feel is pain, and that pain is just the way life is, is it even still pain?

Amazing thing about life, things can be so bad, but you live anyway. Your heart keeps pumping even if you wish it would stop. You just go in some place in your head where nobody can find you, and you hide yourself away.

I'd go there all the time and think of my mother and she'd seem so real when I was with her in my thoughts. And I'd pray alone, and pray for her to come and get me, and I could hear her voice calling me. And then that's all I wanted, to be with her. And I'd just ignore the pain, and wait until it stops.

The thing about pain is, if you ignore it, it goes away. And then you're free. That's the kind of free I was. I didn't care if I lived or died. That's where I lived. Didn't care anymore. My life meant nothing to me. And that's what made me stronger.

So when I come home late from playing basketball and my grandpa cracks my head against the wall until I bleed for being late, that's just pain I know by now, and I don't really feel it anymore.

And when my uncles, all three, beat on me until I'm bloody and my body is screaming pain, and I lie on the floor and I can't move, and they're still kicking on me, then that's just what I know. But I don't feel it anymore.

When they hit you for bleeding, when they beat you for

crying, when they kick you if you don't get up and be a man, then that's just what you do. You get up again. What's left?

And so now there's a monster inside me, and that monster knows, if there's nothing left for them to take, they don't have any more power.

So when they beat me, I get up and I come right back at them. And if they beat me again, I get up again. And again.

And I say, "That didn't hurt. What you gonna do now?"

If they think they're really showing me now, and they think that I can't take no more, and that they finally won, then I just come back again and lick the blood from my hands and say, "What else you got? Is that all?"

I knew I wasn't gonna stop them. I knew there was no way to avoid this pain. So I came back, came back at 'em, back again, and back for more. They had to kill me and I didn't care if they did. It didn't matter any more. My mom was in heaven waiting for me. So you could do what you wanted. I wouldn't back down. And I wouldn't listen. I wouldn't do what you said. And I wouldn't be disciplined anymore. I wouldn't be told by nobody.

They exhausted themselves hitting me, but I wouldn't stay down.

They all saw it then. They all got it.

My uncles saw it and my grandpa saw it. Uncle Oliver slams me down one night and every time he did I just come up again. And he's laughing and he's hitting me, and thinks it's funny how I fall down. And I go down on the floor and come right back up. And he's hitting me more, but I come right back up again.

And he's saying, "Look at Johnny. He's a pit bull, man. He don't back down."

They all saw it then and they all laughed. Laughed how bloody I was, laughed how I couldn't stand up straight, laughed how I wouldn't give up. But I kept coming, and if they smacked me down, I got up anyway.

And then I heard them talking about me. And I heard the pride and the praise in their words, and I recognized it as the love that I wanted so bad, and I needed so bad, and I missed so much.

And from then on I learned how to get that love. Because that's all I really wanted. I don't care who you are. Everybody needs to feel love.

6

I BECAME A FIGHTER ON A FRIDAY NIGHT IN THE SUMMER OF 1975. I was nine years old. We were hanging at Wells Park Community Center, me, with my uncles and cousins beside me, and a ghetto gang from Martinez Town, come to make some trouble.

Actually they came to play basketball, and we all played a game. That was the way it always went. A rival gang claiming Martinez Town or Barelas, Trumbull or Kirtland, La Mesa or Alamosa, would come and challenge Wells Park to a basketball game. And the game would go on good and guys would drink beers, or whiskey from paper bags stashed in their cars or in the bushes. Or they'd snort coke in the bathrooms, or tie up behind the building, and they'd all be flying like kites and angry and pissed and stupid and trash talking and playing to the death, and someone would eventually throw an elbow or get somebody in the eye with a jab, or someone would shove a guy from the other gang and make him fall and he'd leap up pissed, and a huge brawl would come out of it and end the game with everybody throwing punches 'til somebody came and broke the whole thing up.

On one of those nights, it was guys from Martinez town playing with Wells Park, and me and Oliver and Randall and Raymond are there. And we're playing and some bad dude hits Oliver, and Oliver shoves him kinda rough, and the guy pulls a knife. But I jump up and I get in between them. I'm saying, "Come on, man. That's my brother, man. You wanna kill somebody, you gotta kill me first." And the guy's about two feet taller than me and he's looking down at me like I'm probably in kindergarten, and he looks at Randall, "You got your little brother takin' care of business for you, man? You're a pussy, man, got a pussy standin' up for you."

But now I'm pissed and I shove the guy, and Randall grins and says, "He's no pussy, bro. He's a pitbull, man. Nobody fights like him, man. You gotta see him."

Now they're all laughing. See, no matter what age I'm at, my uncles and my cousins, they're all six foot, six one, and I'm the only short one.

"He don't even come up to your tits, cabron. Are you fucked in the head?"

And Randall's going, "Bet you five bucks, he can fight any one of you guys.'

They look at each other. They look at me. They almost don't bother.

"You're fucked."

"Five bucks, man. Anybody. Take him on. He'll kick your ass. Come on."

I'm watching this, like they're talking about somebody else. There's a funny feeling in my gut, a big feeling of pride, and

I'm looking at Randall and all I can feel is love for the guy.

They all shrug, "Okay."

One of the big guys takes off his shirt. I take off my shirt.

They all make a circle and now I'm walking, my hands held up like I seen my grandpa do it hundreds of times, up behind the shed, hitting that punching bag. The Martinez guys are laughing and calling me a piece of shit pussy.

And I'm staring at the guy, walking in a circle. He's got a shaved head and tattoos on his arms, and he looks stoned and mad and ready. And then there's something that happens in my head. There's a moment something snaps. It's like one moment I can smell the dirt and the baking concrete and the beer on his breath, and I can hear their voices around me, everybody yelling and trash talking, and then all of a sudden I don't hear nothing no more. I don't see nothing, I don't feel nothing, nothing except this superpower growing inside, this feeling like I'm gonna die anyway so there's nothing left to lose. And I start to lay in on this guy, and he doesn't even know what hit him, I'm so fast. I'm kicking and biting and punching, and I'm about half his size, and that makes me faster and meaner, and I hit him in the gut so many times before he can even find me that he's on the ground moaning, writhing before the whole thing is over and the Martinez guys are shaking their heads and counting out five one dollar bills in Randall's hand.

Oliver and Raymond are pounding me on the back, laughing and bellowing in my ear.

"Alright, J.T! Good job, Johnny!"

Mi Vida Loca

And I am looking at them kind of confused, my eyes all wide, all proud, the world slowly fading back in. And I'm seeing their grinning faces and feeling their hands on my shoulders and I think I never felt so good. Randall comes up and hands me a dollar bill and he punches me for fun, and I got a grin from ear to ear and I can hear my own voice echoing inside my head, and I'm yelling at them like I'm deaf, "You like that? I showed him, huh? I showed him! You see that? I showed him, man!" And they're nodding, and snorting laughs, and slapping me on the back.

When we come home, my grandpa doesn't beat me for fighting. He sits down at the table in the kitchen, drinking his whiskey and squeezing his hand strengthener real slow, flexing his jaw as he hears my uncles tell him about my fight. And then he grins at me and calls me over and throws me a few punches himself.

"You're my boy, huh, Johnny. I made you tough. All those times I cracked your head on the wall. You're a tough guy now, huh, Johnny? Your grandpa made you tough."

So from then on, Friday nights, my uncles take me to Wells Park, or to the corner in front of the Allsup's by the alley, or in front of Garcia's Kitchen, and they put me up to fight anybody that comes. I'm like a circus act, and I make them look real good. They bring on anybody to fight me and I better win.

If I win I get a dollar and a pat on the back. If I lose, my uncles beat me so bloody, its worse than anybody else is ever gonna to do me. So, pretty soon I'm not losing anymore. It wasn't worth losing. And now I'm winning every time, beating anybody that comes my way, anybody at all, getting a reputation.

My grandpa Miguel now looks at me more and more, studies me over the breakfast table, looking at my black eyes and my red swollen cheeks, like he's thinking about something in his head.

Then one day he pulls me behind the shed and puts me in front of the punching bag and he says, "Go ahead. Take a punch at it, Johnny. You can fight. You can be a fighter."

I take a few punches and he pushes me aside and he shows me how to do it right.

"Here, Johnny. You wanna keep your feet like this. Your shoulder comes with you, like this. Bam. You see? Bam. Bam." He's hitting the bag and I swear I can hear his knuckles breaking.

Then he puts me to the bag again, and I start to hit it, and I start to hear him talking to me, and I start to get it. So I'm punching the bag, faster and faster. And he stands by, watching, his fingers jingling the change in his pockets and watches me proud, with a smile around his eyes.

"Life is a fight, hito," he says. "And you got the fight. You got the fight in you."

Now I start to hang with my grandpa all the time. And that man was my hero. I idolized him.

He always got up every morning at 4:45 and went running only now I'm running with him. He never gained an ounce in all his life. He told me over and over. Was the same weight

Mi Vida Loca

since he was a fighter back before the mines. He loved his strength and his body and took his vitamins every day and drank a health shake every day. I wanted to be just like him.

Every morning we drive in his old yellow pick up truck and pull up beside the Rio Grande by Mountain Avenue, and it's still dark but me and him, we go run. His black lung always bothers him in the end, but he never quits, and I keep up as best as I can.

I hit the bag every day behind the shed with him watching me. After school, I don't go home, I go to the Convention Center where he works his janitor job, and I help wheel the buckets out of the closets and through the hallways, and I haul the mops across the floors and I even scrub the urinals and change the blue tint tablets in the toilet bowls just to help him out.

And on Friday nights we both stay late and watch the wrestling shows from the top of the bleachers. I loved looking down at that ring under the lights. And afterwards he takes me in the dressing room and I look at all the big guys, their muscles bulging huge, their bodies big and strong, and I watch my grandpa joking with them all, and I love him even more.

I was nine years old. Then my grandpa gets the idea to take me to a boxing show to make me enter as a fighter. He said I was good. He said I was ready. And I was. There was nothing I wanted more than to be a boxer like my grandpa.

So on a Sunday night, we're at the Rotary Club up on Central and Juan Tabo, where they're sponsoring a lot of amateur fights.

He enters me himself, writes in my name. I'm wearing a pair of hand me down shorts from my uncles, and right before the fight my grandpa had me drink five milk shakes to add ten pounds of liquid.

There's a man smoking a cigar, weighing people, and he calls me.

"Tapia, is there a Tapia?"

I step forward. He looks me up and down.

"What are you, five years old?"

"I'm nine."

"You gotta weigh seventy pounds."

I nod and he points me to the scale.

I get on and keep my hands over the pockets of my shorts to hide the rocks my grandpa stuffed inside them just to make me a little heavier still.

The man looks at the scale like he doesn't believe me. And then he makes a note on his clipboard and says, "Okay. Tapia. You're in. Get in back and wait your turn. Next."

My grandpa stands with me as we watch the other fights, and he's rubbing my shoulders and telling me to go get in there and kill the next guy I see.

So when it's my turn, I get in the ring and start to run around some scrawny, tall kid like I wanna knock him over with my back draft I'm creating by running so much. I can hear people laughing. He waits and then comes at me all of a sudden and corners me, and he's just trying to hit me while I'm dancing back and forth. Finally he comes close enough to make contact and I forget everything my grandpa taught me, and all my street shit kicks in and I'm wailing at him, punching him, kicking him, biting him. And the man with the cigar waves his hands and stops the fight and tells me to go home. Says I'm just a street fighter. Tells me I can't fight again until I'm eleven.

We drive home in the yellow truck that night and I don't get any tortillas for a week.

7

IT WAS TWO LONG YEARS I WAITED TO BECOME A REAL BOXER.

I fought on street corners for money and praise. I beat up bullies in school. I took beatings for other kids, just 'cause it didn't bother me. I protected any kid who was being picked on. I was a kind of Robin Hood for any kid who needed protection.

Kids in school loved me. Teachers sent me home. I had a mouth on me that didn't shut up. And every night I had nightmares, and woke up screaming, waking my grandparents. I was a crazy ball of energy, bouncing all over the place.

Come summer my grandparents try to take a break from me and my cousin Alfred, and send me and Randall and Raymond to my Auntie Charlotte's trailer down in El Paso, Texas. She had no electricity and no running water. So we'd go out and kick the dirt by the river, or throw tumbleweeds or look for snakes or collect dead birds.

Seems like all we ate was rice. Three times a day it was rice. My Aunt Charlotte had nothing much. She was nice enough, but it was hard for her.

Mi Vida Loca

The trailer didn't have a toilet or a shower, so we had to walk down through the mesquite and pee on the cactus. We'd take baths in the Rio Grande. It was an ugly, muddy, dirty river by the time it got down to El Paso, but we thought it was fun.

The Rio Grande is right across from Juarez, Mexico. You could see cardboard shacks on the hills on the other side where people lived, and my Auntie Charlotte's trailer looked like a mansion.

One day we all were throwing water on our backs in the river, getting clean, and Alfred starts teasing me about how I can't swim.

"Shut up. I can too swim."

"The hell, you can, Johnny."

"Oh yeah? Race me across."

I must have been dizzy in the head from heat, or just being a crazy kid. I wade out.

"Look at me! I'm swimming!"

I'm walking in the muddy ground, pretending to swim, and suddenly I hit a sinkhole and lose my footing, and I drop under and get sucked down deep by a whirlpool.

It sucks me down so far, I feel I'll never get back up. The current takes me away and I'm going in and out of the water, hollering, gulping dirty water and air, until I don't remember anything, and I get caught under a bridge and the migras haul me out on the Mexican side, unconscious.

They thought I was dead for a moment. Some border patrol gives me mouth to mouth and revives me. Then they drive me home in their border patrol jeep. It was the third time in my life I could have been dead, but I wasn't.

Aunt Charlotte sends me back to my grandparents right quick. Says I'm too much trouble. But I'm glad to go home, 'cause I sure missed that toilet we had.

Back in Albuquerque, my uncles and cousins are all spending time at the gym in Wells Park, learning how to box with Henry Anaya Sr. He set up a ring in the community center and called it "Henry's Gym." Grandpa has me train there, too.

Night after night we all go and train and box there. Tapias are getting a reputation as fighters. Five Tapias training there. You didn't mess with us. I'm the little one, but nobody's got my speed, and Henry Anaya Sr. notices it, and he often tells me so.

The week I turn eleven, Grandpa takes me to go fight. We get in the yellow truck, me in my ragged shorts and my gloves. And he keeps talking in on me all the way there.

"Remember what I taught you, Johnny. You're a boxer. Not a street fighter. You box like your grandpa. You don't kick."

"I got it, Grandpa. Don't you worry."

"Use your hands. Use your body. Use your control. You use your skills."

"I will, Grandpa."

"Don't make me a fool now."

"I won't, Grandpa."

"Just remember how I taught you, hito."

"I remember, Grandpa."

We're at a high school gym. Kiwanis Club sponsoring the fight night. Ten guys are fighting. I look for an opponent and pick the biggest guy in the room.

Grandpa is shaking his head.

"Come on, Johnny."

"I can take him, Grandpa. Let me fight him."

"Why you gotta pick him, hito?"

"I can take him. I know it. I wanna fight him."

"He's the biggest guy here."

"That's why I wanna fight him, Grandpa."

So grandpa signs me in, loads down my pockets with rolls of quarters. I get weighed, pass weight, and I'm in the fight.

The gym is half full, and people are yelling and cussing and hollering, looking for some action.

I get in the ring, and face this huge kid with a shaved head. The bell rings and I start dancing all over the place, jabbing the air. And I can see him coming at me. And for a moment time gets really slow. All I can see is his eyes, his big open nostrils. He's a real ugly guy, and some feeling starts to come up from deep down inside me, and it's all a feeling in slow motion. I was so trained by then, that if you face an opponent, you gotta fight to the death. I loved that one on one combat. Who's the better man? May the better man stay standing. So I'm dancing around this guy and all I can think and feel deep in my gut is that I want to kill him or else I'm gonna die.

The whole thing takes forty seconds. I hit the guy so hard

and so fast, he never even got out a punch on me. My fists are so quick, he never could answer my speed. I catch him on the chin with a left and next thing, he's doubled over and down on the mat. I'm so crazy I don't even know the guy is down, and I'm still punching. I win it with the KO in under a minute

My first win. My first trophy. I thought I won a billion dollars, man. Woo!

Once it started that way, it just went that way. I trained at Henry's and trained with my grandpa. And I get more and more fights and more and more wins.

My grandpa was now retired from the city and he starts making it like his work is to train me and support me, taking me from fight to fight.

Both of us together, we drive in the yellow pick up truck, and he's always quiet on the way to the fight. And then I win the match. And on the way back he's talking a lot, and saying, "You're just like me, Johnny. You're a champ. Just like your old grandpa."

My brothers are all boxing, too. Randall, Raymond, Oliver, Steven. Old Henry Anaya, he was a life long trainer, and he had set up his gym for street kids, to train them, and encourage them, wanting to make a difference, giving kids a way out of the barrio. It was now called "Henry's Boxing Club" and it started to grow and bring in a lot of kids. His own son is training there. And we all went to regionals and fought together a lot. Me and my brothers.

Every one of them had had some training from my grandpa. Every one had some dream of being a champion one day.

Mi Vida Loca

And my brothers are having fights and having pretty good success too.

Half the time, I drove Henry crazy, running around the gym, jumping up and down, talking a mile a minute. He liked me, but I drove him crazy.

I'd come in the gym with my voice I can't keep quiet. I'm not real shy.

"Hey, Henry! How's it going?!"

"Hey, Johnny."

"You doin' good tonight?"

"Doin' good, Johnny."

"That's good, boss. Real good!"

"You gonna train tonight, Johnny? Or you gonna run around like a monkey?"

He's just kidding. And I liked to kid back. I was never a quiet kid, always lit up, but now I'm all lit up with confidence, too. Always talking, joking, all my energy rubbing off on everybody else in the gym.

I was just the guy looking for love wherever I could find it. Boxing gave me that love from the beginning. From the dollar bill and the pat on the back from my brothers, to my first trophy, and all the time I spent with my grandpa. I was in an element that was just right for me. And I love people and it put me around people all the time. I was always hugging everybody in the gym. Talking with my cousins. Winning fight after fight in front of a loud crowd, loving the cheers of that audience.

Sometimes I joked so much, people didn't take me seriously. Only my grandpa really knew how serious I was. He put all his time and belief in me. He was proud of his whole family, all his sons and nephews, but he always said to me, "You got something special, Johnny. You're just like me. You're gonna be a champ." He made me believe in myself.

Me and him, we're out there every weekend, driving all over New Mexico, Farmington, Carlsbad, Gallup, and Clovis. I'm winning tournaments, winning trophies and ribbons.

I win so much, we start to go out of state to regionals. Sometimes it's Henry Anaya's van. A lot of times it's my grandpa driving. We drive to Colorado, Arizona, Texas, Utah. We logged more miles in that yellow pick up. My grandpa's always got the Mex tunes on the radio. He loved all the old school Mexican stuff, Vicente Fernandez, Pedro Infante, and, of course, El Godfather of New Mexico, Al Hurricane. And if I won by knockout, he'd be real happy on the way home and bellow out "Madrecita, Te Debo Tanto!" real loud.

I won so many trophies, my grandpa clears out the shed behind the house, takes a broom to the thing, and sweeps and mops it for a whole day. I help him hammer a big shelf together from scrap wood. He files and sands it and paints it nice. It's all to keep my trophies up, he's that proud of me.

It was a good time for me and him. It was a good time in my life, period. I'd do anything for my grandpa then and now. And he did everything for me. He and my grandma even made it official and adopted me. Grandpa and Grandma Ester became my legal parents. We never talked about it. Never talked about my mom. Never made a big deal out of it. But they wanted it to be right. They wanted me to belong. And I loved them with all my heart for it.

My uncles and cousins sometimes let on to feeling some jealousy. There was a lot of talk from my Aunt Helen to my grandpa about how there's other fighters in the house, namely Steven, and he's the one who never fought all that good. But he was her baby. Oliver was a good fighter, and even won a Golden Glove. Never got a trophy shrine, though. They were all good, my brothers, but I had my grandfather behind me.

One night we were driving home after a fight that I won. My grandpa is in one of his moods to talking.

"You're a champ, hito. Just like your old grandpa."

We talked about the fight. About what we were gonna get for dinner. If it was gonna be red or green chili. It was one of the happiest moments I can remember.

As we were driving, some pick up truck comes up and cuts my grandpa off, making him veer on the shoulder of the highway.

He's pissed and he's red in the face.

"You see that?!"

"I saw it."

"He cut me off, cabron!"

So he drives after them real fast and gets next to them and cuts them off the road and forces them into the dirt.

"You get' em, Johnny! You show them! Show 'em they can't disrespect your old grandpa!"

And I go and do it. I didn't want to do it. But I knew that's what my grandpa wanted. I had to defend his honor. I knew he was counting me.

The guy in the front seat just looks at me confused while I'm pulling him out of the car and onto the pavement. I pull him into the street and pound on him 'til he cowers and whimpers, begging. The other guy in the car looks like he's praying. I leave him alone, get back in the truck and we drive the rest of the way home like nothing happened.

We don't say anything about it. Don't need to say anything. He knows I'll do anything for him. Anything he needs. I know he asked me to do that because he's proud of me. Because he needs me. 'Cause if I do that for him, he will love me. He will never say it. He'll never say the word love. But there are many ways to say it. He'll throw punches at me all day long. That was just his way of saying "I love you." He'll drive me to all the fights. Run with me every morning. That was his way. He was a proud man. A real traditional man. Fiercely proud and proud of me. He meant everything to me back then.

The trophies start to be so many now, my grandpa built more shelves. And he was proud of those trophies, man, like he won them himself. It became like a Vatican altar in there. I got more than a few nasty looks from the others in the house.

Oliver and Randall start saying, "Don't come home if you lose, Johnny." They laugh, but I know they meant it.

I had gone from the runt of the house, to the champion, the one favored by my grandpa. I'd get hassled, but they all knew better. They couldn't beat me to the edge of my life anymore. They had to watch me go out and win. And I loved them all, but I wasn't crying for them. It was their own fault. They created the monster in the first place.

8

THEY SAY YOU CAN TAKE THE FIGHTER OUT OF THE STREETS, BUT YOU CAN'T TAKE THE STREETS OUT OF THE FIGHTER.

Maybe it's true.

Boxing is a way out of the streets for those who have no other way in life, for those who are poor, and there are plenty of them in the barrio in Albuquerque. You just need a pair of shorts and some gloves and the desire to beat your anger and frustration out on somebody else and get paid for it. What could be better? If people asked me why I liked boxing, I used to joke that boxing was the only way I could hit somebody and not go to jail.

Boxing became my life. I went to school. I went to fights. In school I was a star. I never went hungry, kids always giving me some of their lunches, because everybody wanted to be my friend. I got respect and nobody messed with me. I did well in school, too, got good grades, even though I didn't tell anybody at home. For my grandpa, getting good grades was not manly. You went to school because the law required it, that's all. So I hid my grades, hid my smarts.

I became a kid living on two sides of life. And one side was always hidden from the other, and one side often contradicted the other, and I'm probably still that way.

Part of it is I always made no difference between people. From the highest to the lowest, we all got two hands and two feet. When you're high and I'm low. When you're low and I'm up on a mountain. Makes no difference. I don't see people different that way.

And another part of it was, that no matter how civilized I got by the success, no matter how many opportunities success provided for me, the streets never left me, even after I left them.

The streets had fed me and trained me and brought me up. They had nearly destroyed me, they had taken my mother, but they also had my back, they also had protected me and been loyal to me. They've been imprinted too deep. I've died too many times. I've seen too many people die.

That pull is always there.

Without my mother around, I was thrown into the world of the streets. I grew up with people older than me, with people who were in and out of prison. I grew up with heroin addicts, and drug dealers, and murderers. These were normal people to me. They laughed with you. Did you a favor. Accepted you. These were people from the streets, people that claimed Wells Park, like me, people in gangs, people from desperate places.

Death was everywhere. Life meant very little. Every day was about survival. It was like living in a constant war zone.

Violence is power. Lawlessness is survival.

I saw people die all the time.

My partner, Anthony Padilla, cops shot him right in front of me at Pat Hurley Park. We were fighting. He pulled a knife on me, cops saw it and shot him in the head. Then they came and told me the bullet wasn't meant for him, that they were aiming for me. I watched him die right there.

My partner, Roger, hanged himself in jail.

My partner, Nathan, was in the Crips and the Bloods were after him. He was begging me, calling, "Help me, Johnny, help me." There was nothing I could do. They shot him. He died in front of me.

My partner, Ernie Sandoval, axed in the head at Dennis Chavez Park.

And there were guys who tried to do right.

I had a partner, Victor Salazar, my best friend in high school; I really loved this guy. He went ROTC in his senior year, tried to get me to go. He was all full of ideas, didn't want to end up on the streets, in crime, like everybody else. He joined the Navy. They made him handle the canons. But the bombs were old. Exploded right on top of him. Tore his body to pieces. Tore me up, too. You do right and you die just the same. Too much death all around me.

That kind of life leaves its mark on anyone. And it left its mark on me. Everything is measured by life and death. Everyone lives by the law of the streets.

Number one rule: "You don't rat."

You rat and you fall from grace in the streets. You see a

partner commit a double murder, you don't say anything. What happens in the streets stays in the streets. You see people kill, strangle, stab, you don't rat.

The enemy is police. The enemy is society. You're out on the street doing illegal things. You're selling guns. They want to stop you. They are the enemy.

You do illegal things because that is your survival. You don't have money. You don't have an education. They have it all. You got nothing. They have the advantage. You're just doing what you can. Society owes you your survival. This is how the street thinks.

Raised in that environment, you learn to break the rules. You don't trust police. You don't trust anyone. Society sets the rules. You need to break them.

They want to stop you from doing what you want to do. They feel superior. They think you're inferior if you're poor, if you live on food stamps and assistance. They think, "Why don't you just get off your butt and work?" So you steal because you don't want to take from the government. You got pride.

You defend your family. You don't rape someone else's family member. There is a code among thieves. You don't break into homes of the other families. You are loyal. You have family values. Family is everything. You walk the streets of Wells Park and you know you're safe, because you belong.

Lee Montoya was a kid who was like another brother to me. Still is. His mother was a drug addict. Gave him away to his grandparents. He had known the pain. And had nowhere to belong to like me, and my grandparents allowed him to be a part of our lives as though he was another son to them. He was always at the house.

Years later, when Raymond was attacked by a rival gang member on neutral turf, Raymond stabbed him twenty two times and killed him. Raymond got away, but the gang retaliated. They drove by my grandparents' house looking for him and shot the place up. My grandma was in the kitchen and fell to the floor. She was miraculously unhurt. Then they found Raymond and bashed his brains in until he almost died in the hospital.

Lee was family. Lee was loyal. He took care of it. He knew the guy who did it. He took a sawed off shot gun to his face and killed him.

Lee went to prison.

My grandparents love him for that to this day.

He was loyal.

A guy named James later ratted on Raymond, and Raymond went to prison for second-degree murder.

I found James and gave him shit for ratting. I got charged with intimidating a witness. Almost went to prison for it, too.

These things took place over years. But this was a part of my life for a long time, and it has never really let me go, no matter how far, and to what heights boxing has taken me.

So when I was sent to the Junior Olympics in my high school amateur days, I ended up getting kicked out of the training camp because me and my roommate, Mike Tyson, the hugest, shyest guy you ever met, we, and a couple of

Mi Vida Loca

Samoans at our side, got into it with some guys in a bar outside of camp. We broke the rules. All of us kicked out. Bad news.

"Johnny, you better stay out of trouble."

"Johnny, you better hold it together."

"Johnny, stay away from those guys."

I never wanted trouble. I was never in the middle of it. It was never something I started. I was never a hood. I wanted to belong. I want to belong to something.

But I also kept outside of it all.

I was the only person who claimed Wells Park who could go anywhere else in town and not be bothered. I could go to Martinez Town, to Barelas, to SanJo, to Trumbull. Nobody messed with me. Everybody welcomed me. It was different for me. I knew the law of the street, I knew how to survive, but I knew I had other things in store. And I knew I wanted more.

I straddled both sides for a long time. The glory and the infamy. The brothers were always calling me to be there for them. If they needed me, I was there. But I had another life, a life that was lifting me up. Boxing was bringing me into the world. Boxing gave me a chance to get out.

The Maloof family made the biggest difference in my early boxing life. They were really the ones to lift me out of the streets and give me new hopes and dreams.

They were the Coors distributors in New Mexico. Good people, with good values. Their kids went to my high school.

They gave me so much. They helped support my family, helped me get a car. They paid for airfare to fights. They gave me a job on the keg route, hauling beer kegs for Coors, hauling kegs before the fights because rolling those big ass kegs of beer in and out of the trucks would keep me real conditioned. It was a job and training all in one.

Colleen Maloof, the mom, she was a sweet, beautiful woman, so generous, so loving. Loved me like a son. She always put it into my head to follow my dream, to go for the dream of being a world-class boxer. More than anybody else, she always encouraged me.

She welcomed me into her life and into her home. She had me come to the house all the time and swim with her kids. Me and her son, George, we hung out a lot. Hung out with Robbie Unser, too. Bobby Unser's son.

We all went to high school together. George was in my corner many times at fights. Robbie was going through a lot with his dad. We talked a lot about life and family.

Robbie made up a training technique for me with his car. We'd go out on the racetrack and he had me pushing his racecars back and forth to build strength. We had so much fun, the three of us, they called us the "Three Musketeers."

They were from good New Mexico families. Famous families. I was famous myself. They came over and ate my grandma's tamales. I spent so much time at the Maloof's, Colleen started talking about adopting me.

Boxing did a lot for me.

That's what I mean. I sure had a rough start in life. I come from a place that destroys a lot of people. But good things always came into my path. Like somebody was watching over me. Sometimes I think it's my mother. Sometimes I think it's the Good Lord upstairs. So, what am I? The luckiest or the unluckiest one?

Stan Gallup, Boxing Commissioner of New Mexico, and Golden Gloves Board Member got me to the Golden Gloves Championships. I won State Golden Gloves Championships five times, and National Golden Gloves two times, in two different weight classes.

Stan was a good man. Helped me a lot, too. He took me to Finland for the Junior Olympics. Me and Mike Tyson rooming again. Stan says I was robbed in the end, but I gave everybody a break dancing show in the arena, had a bigger audience than the boxing did. They loved me in Finland.

How far is Finland from the ghetto? A whole miracle away.

9

"DON'T QUIT."

When things go wrong as they sometimes will,
 when the road you're trudging seems all up hill,
when funds are low and the debts are high,
 and you want to smile but you have a sigh,
when care is pressing you down a bit,
rest if you must, but
"Don't Quit."

Life is queer with its twists and turns,
as every one of us sometimes learns,
 and many a failure turns about,
when he might have won had he stuck it out.
Don't give up though the pace seems slow,
you may succeed with another blow.
Success is failure turned inside out,
the silver tint of the clouds of doubt,
and you never can tell how close you are,
it may be near when it seems so far,
so stick to the fight when you're hardest hit,
it's when things seem worst you must
 "Not Quit!"
(Written on the wall at Barelas Boxing Gym, Albuquerque)

I won so many fights, they called me the "Baby Faced Assassin."

In the ring, I had smarts, speed, and something else that nobody could match. A fury that drove every punch, every cut. I used rage when I saw my opponent. My opponent was my enemy. My opponent was the symbol of death. I wasn't afraid of death, and I had known darkness. I could go to places nobody else had. And they never knew what hit 'em. They tried, but they just couldn't match it.

I looked ten even when I was fifteen, sixteen, seventeen years old. Half the fighters I faced underestimated me. The others were helpless against my speed and my fury. In my amateur years I won one hundredand one fights and only lost twenty one, with sixty five KOs. There was nothing to stop me.

I started training at Barelas Gym. A gym in my old neighborhood known for the fighters it produced. I still ran every day with my grandpa. I was healthy and strong. I was about to graduate from high school and I wanted to turn pro.

I wanted to be champ, like any boxer does. I wanted to be champion of the world. When I was young I admired Sugar Ray Leonard, Julio Cesar Chavez, and Bruce Lee. First time you put on boxing gloves those champions are in your mind and you see yourself up there, wearing the champion's belt one day. Everybody dreams. Everybody wants it. I dreamed it, too. I knew it would happen, believed in it, never questioned that it would happen.

Every day in the gym at Barelas I walked past the big pictures they had of fighters. Posters of fighters in New Mexico like, Bobby Foster and Jim Johnson, and Waldo Anaya. I wanted my picture up there someday.

Paul Chavez was training fighters at San Jose Community Center. He had a reputation for getting pro fighters big fights. I'd bug him all the time to take me. Chavez always said no. Said good amateur doesn't mean good pro. He said he had too many fighters already. He thought I was too hyper and I wasn't focused enough. I made too many jokes. The fact that I hugged him every time I saw him might have had something to do with it. I just wasn't getting anywhere with him.

My grandpa didn't think I needed anybody.

"You got me, don't you? You got Henry at the boxing club. What do you need?"

"I need a trainer. I need a manager. I wanna be champ."

"You'll be champ."

"I gotta train with Paul Chavez."

"Chavez? What's he got that I don't got? That Henry don't got? What's he know that you don't know already?"

"He puts on pro fights, Grandpa. He's got real fighters. I love you, Grandpa, but I gotta have somebody real.

"Are you sayin' I'm not real?"

"I'm not saying that, Grandpa."

"You don't need Chavez. You're a pro already. You got it all. You can do it yourself."

But I knew I couldn't. I had to get to the next level. And you need somebody who can get you in the ring.

Colleen Maloof was always pushing me to follow my

dream to become a pro fighter. She finally pulled some strings and arranged for me to train with Beto Martinez in Phoenix, Arizona. I bugged my grandpa until he said it was okay for me to go.

The Maloofs paid the airfare. They set up a hotel room for me. And I'm supposed to wait for Beto to come and get me. I wait for three days. I stare at the phone. I watch TV. Day becomes night and day again. Nobody comes.

Something happened, sitting in that room alone, waiting alone. I start thinking, thinking too much maybe. Thinking about thirteen straight years of boxing. Thinking about how tired I was. Thinking about how disappointed I was that nothing was happening, that all my work left me waiting in a hotel away from home.

What happened? All those years winning, all that press, voted "most interesting fighter to watch." So, what was wrong? It seemed like I couldn't get anybody to take me on. How could that be after all that work and all that praise and all that success? Suddenly, the whole thing looked stupid. And I was feeling stupid, sitting there at this hotel, waiting by the phone, watching TV. And those voices start to come into my head. And all the voices of praise start to get drowned out by other voices: "You're nothing. You're never gonna be nothing. You're stupid, Johnny. This whole thing is stupid, Johnny. You ain't goin' nowhere. You're no good."

Problem is, if you got too much time on your hands, you start thinking too much. Way too much.

Beto shows on the fourth day. Takes me to his gym. But

he wasn't going to be training me.

Some other guy takes over, starts telling me what to do. And I don't like the way he does things. And he don't like the way I do things. And he's criticizing everything move I make, and I'm thinking, thirteen years I been fighting, one hundred and fifty wins, I know what I'm doing. And now I'm here in this stinkin' hot desert with this guy I don't like. This is it? And I'm thinking, I don't wanna do this. I don't wanna be away from my family. I don't wanna be in one hundred degree Arizona away from everybody I know. My brothers, my two Musketeers, my grandpa, my partners on the street. I was just feeling lost. I was a desert rat from Albuquerque. I didn't get the palm trees and the golf courses. I just didn't feel right in Phoenix. I just wasn't ready.

I went back home to Albuquerque and stopped fighting. Gave the whole thing up. After thirteen long years. After being orphaned, taken in and beaten within an inch of my life, after having nothing left to lose, finding my survival, and finding the love I lost in becoming a fighter, fighting on street corners, in the gym, in the ring, all over the world. After all that I ever knew was fighting. After literally fighting for my life, I gave it all up. Didn't set foot in the gym again. Didn't touch a bag. Not a glove. Never ran along the Rio Grande. Never jumped a rope. I was tired, burned out on the whole thing to be honest. Thirteen years of fighting without a stop. Guess I stopped knowing if I really wanted to do it all. It had become something I had to do, forgot if I wanted to do it. So I stopped it all. Stopped fighting. For two years. I quit.

10

MY GRANDMA ESTER USED TO SAY, "WALK CAREFULLY THROUGH LIFE, HITO. YOU NEVER KNOW WHERE THE GHOSTS ARE BURIED."

She had a way of putting things, had a way of hinting at all the bad out there, you always felt it could come knocking at your door any moment.

She was very superstitious, and her superstitions were all meant to keep the bad away. Like you could have control.

You'd drop a knife on the floor, she'd say you've got to pick it up, rinse it with cold water and make the sign of the cross over it, or someone will die.

You'd find a coin tails up, she'd say, "Don't pick it up. It's bad luck."

She'd never let anybody cut their nails on a Sunday. Never let anybody take her picture because the person standing in the middle would die first.

She wouldn't eat at other people's houses because they could put a spell on you. If someone stared at you they could give you the evil eye. If you stare at a baby too much, you can give it the evil eye, so you have to put a cross on its head to protect it.

Mi Vida Loca

There was always a sense of doom. Always the feeling that something bad was just around the corner.

There was more superstition than religion in that house. My grandparents were deeply Mexican at heart in that way. They had the mixed blood of the Aztecs and the Spanish. If there was a problem, they didn't go to church. They'd go to the curandera. They tried to cure many of their kids from the evil addiction of drugs and alcohol with Mexican witchcraft. Never worked.

I'm living at home but I'm not fighting anymore, and my uncles and cousins have moved out and moved on, many of them right into lives of drugs and crime in the streets. Many of them had been thrown out of the house before they were ready. My grandpa was strict. He didn't tolerate you screwing up. You didn't make the cut, you were out. Just like that. Overnight. Your clothes on the sidewalk.

Everybody rebelled against the strictness at home, took off, and ran right into trouble in the streets. Their lives were empty, without any direction, without love. But I had had too much purpose for that kind of trouble. Boxing had kept me too busy. I got the love through boxing, through winning every week. I hadn't had the time for trouble.

Raymond was in jail. Had already nearly been killed in a gang fight. Crucita had been out and was back in again for heroin. When she had gotten out she took all the kids with her for a while. Moved them into fleabag motels and sent the kids out begging for food while she and her man were shooting up in the motel room. That didn't last long. Oliver was in jail. My oldest uncle, Richard, was at home, but he's a long time heroin addict who's already got nineteen years of jail time behind him for murder.

My Grandma Ester is just so happy to have her son back, she's putting up with anything from him. And he sits on the couch at night, stoned out of his mind from the heroin in his bloodstream, his eyes half shut, his mouth open, drooling, his cigarette hanging through his fingers, slowly reaching for the couch.

I say, "Come on, Grandma. Look at him. All he's doing is burning your couches. Look at him Grandma. Look at the way he is. Why do you put up with him?"

But my grandma, she loved all her children. She could be the harshest, toughest woman I ever met. But you could never say a thing about her children. She was loyal to the bone.

She said, "He's sick, hito. He's sick."

"Is that what you call sick? Look at that."

I was mad at what he did. I couldn't stand what was going on in our family, in the streets, everywhere. I hated seeing him like that.

She said, "One of these days it might happen to you, hito, and then you'll find out. Let's hope it never does. But he's an addict. And you never, never make fun of an addict. Some day it could be you, and you could be worse."

"Not me, Grandma. That's never gonna be me. I got too much to do with my life."

I remember how I thought what she was saying was crazy. I hated drugs. I couldn't understand how people wanted to ruin their lives. I saw so many people in pain. I saw that pain close up. I didn't judge them, I didn't turn them in. At Wells Park they used to ask me to help them shoot up. I had a good grip from boxing and I'd squeeze their arms with my bare hands and make the veins pop. I saw them put those needles in. But I never understood it.

"Next thing you know, it could be you, and you're worse."

My grandma would say those things and it was like she knew she was right. And you could hear the truth in her words, even though you didn't want to. She'd make some point and then leave it alone. But the way she said it, it always had a heavy sound to it, like a prophecy or a curse. I tried to argue. She made me nervous when she got like that. But she wouldn't say any more because she just knew.

I was working. I liked the routine, liked working hard on the keg route, hauling those kegs. Hanging with George and Robbie. Playing basketball at night. Handed over every extra dime to my grandfather to help support the family. He let me have twenty dollars and took the rest. I'd spend that on beer. I will admit, I did drink a few beers in those days.

I had a lot of girls chase me, too, then. Always have. Girls from the streets, girls at the Community Center, girls in the bars. I'd be nice and charming and funny, but I never stuck with anybody. Nice girls, too. I just couldn't be pinned down.

They'd come to the house and be crying, "Is Johnny here? He never calls me no more. Why is he so mean? I thought he loves me."

My grandma would always cover for me, while I'm hiding in the porch.

"He's not here, hita."

They'd cry and leave. She'd look at me when I came back out from hiding, grinning stupid.

"Johnny, what'd those girls do to you?"

"Oh, Grandma, they'll get over it."

"You just wait, Johnny. One of these days you're gonna meet somebody and she's gonna have you so stupid, we're all gonna laugh about it. She's gonna have you all figured out and you're gonna be helpless against her spell. She's gonna have you under so much control and tell you what to do, you're not gonna know what ever happened to you."

I laughed then, too.

There was only one woman on my mind and that was my mother. It was ten years since she died when I graduated from high school and quit boxing. You might think that was a long time to heal. But there was no healing. Her being gone was an open wound. I never closed that hurt off. I had never said good-bye. I had never had any answers. Never any explanation of why she was taken from me.

My mother was buried in the Mount Calvary Catholic Cemetery across the street from my high school. Every morning I walked to school, I walked past that cemetery and saw that grave in the field of graves and flowers. Every day I had played basketball in the schoolyard, I couldn't help but see that cemetery, and feel that grave nearby.

There was no healing, because she was torn away with such violence. Whoever had done this had stabbed her thirty three times. Stabbed her all over her body with a screwdriver and scissors. She had crawled on her belly, crawled bleeding with thirty three stab wounds in her flesh. She didn't want to die. She fought to the end. She had me to come home to. She had a little boy. She loved her life, she loved being alive. She wanted to come home. Ten years later that hurt me as much as it did in the beginning. And it still does today.

I would pace in the house when everybody slept, and I'd be thinking of my mother, and I'd be thinking about who killed her. Who was it? Why did they kill her? Where were they now? Who was the killer?

I started to think that if I found him, I would kill him. I wanted to kill him. I swore if I got the chance I would stab him in the same way he had stabbed my mother. I would make it worse. I wanted him to know what he took away. Took her life away and my life with it, so early. I started asking people questions, asking around. Every time I was out somewhere I would ask, "do you know anything about this?" Every face I looked at, I wondered, "Was this the man?" I wanted him. I wanted that man bad.

At night, I talked to Mom. Walking past that cemetery, I talked to her.

"Hey, Mom. I love you. I miss you. Where are you? Can you hear me?"

Praying at night for her to come and see me, to come and get me. Come be with me. Take me home. There were long nights, I didn't sleep at all. But nobody knew this part of me. I couldn't talk about it. I couldn't do anything with those feelings.

Except in the ring. In the ring those feelings had all been there. All that fury and hate. It had to go somewhere. I had put it all in the ring. It kept me undefeated for many years. It fueled all the wins. My opponent was the man who killed my mother. And I wanted to kill him. And I just knew, some day I would.

But when I stopped fighting these thoughts were in my head more and more, and more and more I started to go down. I'd hang around the house, drive my grandma crazy, eating all her food, making her dance when she wanted to sit down. Making her dance like Virginia used to make her dance. She'd look at me sometimes kind of spooked when I'd dance with her to a song she knew from my mom. Then she'd get quiet and sit down and go back to peeling chiles.

My grandpa finally says, "Johnny. How come you don't go pro? You should go back to boxing."

He was disappointed when I didn't want to box no more. He let me make that decision then. But he always tried.

"Johnny, you're just wasting your time. What are you doing? Get back in that ring. You got the talent, Johnny. Get back to it. You got the stuff."

And he'd throw me some punches and I'd throw them back and roll my head to the side. "I don't know, Grandpa. I quit."

Then I started hearing about a pro fighter training at the South San Jose, "SanJo," Community Center, Mark Perea. Paul Chavez was training him and he was getting some press. Everyone was talking about him and Paul Chavez.

I got too curious. And to be honest, it started to bother me. I was thinking that it should be me. That's what's in the back of my mind. That should be me.

So I went to SanJo and watched the sparring. I paced around in there, and watched Perea train. Watched Paul Chavez train him. I'd stand by the ring and duck and jab along with the sparring.

Then a fighter friend of mine, Tommy Cordova, told me to come and spar with him at SanJo. Tommy was one of four fighting brothers in Albuquerque, Tommy, Ruben, Manuel and Frank. Their father was a trainer and the Cordova's had matched up against me and my brothers in Henry's Boxing Club in tournaments in Albuquerque, so me and him were friends.

Tommy Cordova is a big guy. Huge guy compared to me. I got in the ring with him. I'm half his size. Didn't have a mouthpiece. Just grabbed a napkin and stuffed it in my mouth. Took those gloves and said, "Let's go."

I know Tommy Cordova as a fighter from watching him fight. I know he's a body puncher and I know he's tough. So I know where to stay away from. I also know I got him beat in the speed department. So I start to spar with Tommy and everybody looks nervous for me.

"Come on, Johnny. He's too big for you."

But I know I can do it. And I know Paul Chavez is watching and I let go and let Tommy have everything I got. Paul Chavez watches the whole time, not saying anything, but I could see something in his eyes. He was kind of smiling. The man never smiles actually, but he was watching, and he was impressed.

Tommy Cordova leaves the ring, cursing me like I just went crazy on him, half joking, half mad, and I'm standing there, my chest going up and down, breathing hard.

Chavez comes over. And he's a grouchy old man, for sure. Never cracked a smile. He says in this growly voice, "Okay, Johnny. You be here tomorrow at three. You got some stuff. I'll train you if you wanna get serious."

I jumped out of that ring so fast and hugged that man, which he hated. He's pushing me away.

"No hugging, Johnny."

"I love you, Boss! You gonna take me on!"

"I'm gonna take you on. But you gotta promise me no crazy stuff, Johnny. This is serious. You gotta be serious with me, son. You can't be crazy, alright? You prove yourself, Johnny. You be serious."

"I'm serious. I'm so serious."

I kissed him on the head anyway and turned to everybody in the room.

"I love this man! This is a beautiful human being! Gonna take me on as his fighter!"

I bear hugged him and patted him on the stomach.

"Pablito. Boss man. You won't regret it. I promise you

won't regret it, man."

"Be serious, Johnny, alright?"

"For you, anything. I can be real serious."

Then I threw several kisses to the room, and danced my way out of there, backwards. Last thing I see is Chavez standing there, shaking his head, watching me, wondering what he just done.

11

THE THING ABOUT SUCCESS IS THAT YOU WORK HARD FOR IT EVERY DAY, YOU SACRIFICE FOR IT, YOU DREAM ABOUT IT EVERY MORNING WHEN YOU GET UP AND TRAIN UNTIL YOU GO TO BED, YOUR MUSCLES ACHING. And when success finally comes, when it comes knocking on your door, you can bet you're still standing there in your underwear, and you're not prepared at all.

And then it changes everything.

I had my first fight in Irvine, California. A four round fight my new promoters, Top Rank, put together.

They sent me out on a plane. Paid for Paul, even paid for my grandpa to come. Got me Beto Martinez as my cut man. This was the real thing. It was exciting.

My opponent was a policeman, Efren Chavez. He had eight wins, no losses. For me it was the first time in the ring without headgear. It was strange, and it felt bare. But I fought good, it was a good start, but the fight ended up a draw. I went home and didn't know yet what it all meant.

But two weeks later I had my first significant fight. Back in California, in Fresno this time. I fought a guy named James

Dean and I will never forget this.

He knocked me down in the first round and I hit the canvas hard. It was the only time I ever went down in a fight. Ever.

He got a lucky shot on me and put me down on. I should have been out. I remember the feeling, my legs wobbly, my ears ringing, my head dizzy, spinning, my sides aching, everything's blurry.

My eyes are wide open and confused, and I try to focus again. I can see my grandpa outside the ring, looking up at me. I could see Paul's face. I saw Beto.

I forced myself to get up, and I forced myself to smile. I probably smiled the weirdest smile James Dean ever saw, because I can see him looking at me, like I'm crazy.

The bell rings for the first round and in my corner Beto and Paul think it's all funny, they're pounding on me, hosing me down, grinning, "Welcome to the big time, Johnny."

I let them talk and look at my grandpa on the side. Spit the water in a bucket. Yell out to him so everybody can hear.

"Don't worry, Grandpa. I'll get him."

My grandpa doesn't say anything.

The bell rings. I turn back.

"This is for you, Grandpa."

Then I get back in the ring and I ran right at this James Dean. Right for him, like he might be gone if I don't catch him. I charged him and gave it back to James Dean a hundred times over. I'm grinning like a fool, but I am in fury now. He didn't have a chance. I knocked him down three times to his one, and won it in six rounds.

I was never knocked down again, never in seventeen years of fighting. Never. Not once in fifty eight more fights. Never again.

I won my next five fights by knock out. I kept winning and winning, and people could see right away, there was something going on. The press wrote about it. They brought back my name, "The Baby Faced Assassin." I couldn't be beat.

I fought in Irvine, Las Vegas, Albuquerque, Phoenix. I won fourteen more fights, nine by knock out. People kept talking.

I still hauled the kegs, but my training schedule got so heavy and the purses started paying, pretty soon fighting and training was all that I could do.

One night, a Friday night Fight Night, I am hanging with Tommy Cordova in his trailer. He's the fighter who got me introduced to Paul Chavez. He's been hanging with me more now that I'm pro, too. He had just won his new ESPN belt and me and him were celebrating, days after the fight. I admired him, because he was a champion.

We were watching the fights on TV, and talking boxing, flipping the channels to see if there was any news about him and his belt.

He's got his belt up on a mantle, lit up by a floodlight, and it looks shiny and new.

I am sitting on his couch and I'm looking at this belt, looking at that gold gleaming.

I get up to look at it.

"Can I touch your belt?"

Tommy watches me, grinning.

"Sure. Just don't get your finger prints all over it, man."

"I won't, man. Don't worry."

I run my hands over the gold, and the lettering.

"Can I hold it?"

"Yeah, I guess. But don't mess with it, man. And put it back to where it was."

"Sure, Tommy. I will."

I pick it up and feel how heavy it is. I'm grinning and weighing it with my hands. Lifting it up and down, grinning like a little kid.

"It's heavy, huh?"

He's grinning, too, nodding.

"Yeah, it's heavy. Now put it back."

"Can I put it on?"

"Damn, J.T. Don't mess with it."

"I'm not. I just wanna put it on."

He's trying to frown, but I know he's proud of it.

"Okay, man. Go ahead."

"I'll put it back."

"Okay, okay."

And I put that belt on my waist and feel the weight of it on my body and it feels good.

I grin at Tommy, looking down at the belt, looking up at him.

"One of these days I'm gonna have one of these."

Tommy grins at me, and there's a look in his eyes.

"Yeah, I bet you will. Someday you will, I bet."

And I knew it was true. Some day.

Success. My grandpa was the proudest man. I was a pro. The first in the family. We run every morning. He comes to every fight. He's in the gym all the time. He's by my side.

But with all the success, Paul starts to get possessive. He starts telling my grandpa to stay out of the gym. Paul looks down on my grandpa. Says he doesn't know anything. Says my family is going to keep me down. Says my grandpa's ignorant when it comes to fighting. Doesn't want him telling me anything. Doesn't want him coming to the fights. Says I got to do what's right for my career not for my grandpa. Says he doesn't like distractions when he's training. Doesn't like interference with his methods. He usually never allows other people around his fighters. Says if I want to fight with him, I got to train with him alone. Keep my grandpa out.

I had to tell my grandpa not to come to the gym no more. That hurt me to do that. And it hurt him, too.

"What do you mean? He don't want me there?"

"He says he don't want anybody there when I'm training."

"Who else shows up all the time except me?"

"Nobody, just you."

"Then who's he talking about?"

"He just doesn't want distractions. You know? It's not about you."

"Who else was there since you were a runt? Who else has been training you from the beginning? I'm a distraction? He thinks he's better than me?"

"No, Grandpa. He doesn't think that."

Mi Vida Loca

"Sure he does."

He gets up and goes to the television.

"I still want you to come, you know?"

My grandpa turns on Lawrence Welk, silent.

"You know if it was up to me you'd be there all the time."

He doesn't look at me.

"I love you, Grandpa."

But he's done. It's like I'm not there. No more talking.

Grandpa stops coming to the gym, won't come to the fights. He doesn't talk about it, but his pride has been hurt. Hurt bad. And he is a very proud man.

My Grandma Ester starts talking to me about how I'm selfish and I'm turning my back on my grandpa. How I can just go ahead and have my big professional career, but I'm gonna break my grandpa's heart doing it, and she hopes that's worth it to me.

There was nothing I could say. I just go to the gym and keep working. I go to the fights and keep winning.

I went and got my own apartment. Sun Village Apartments on Locust by Indian School. Still downtown. It's small but I got furniture that I bought myself. I got money in the bank. I got a brand new blue Rally Sport, 1990 model. I'm buying my own groceries, Dr. Pepper, Snickers bars and ice cream. It's all I live on.

I also got my friends hanging with me now. I got partners from the hood, come knocking at my door. I got money now and a place. Everybody wants a piece of me. And it's okay with me.

Some of my partners are doing some drug dealing. I don't do it myself, but I don't judge them for it. They're living on the streets. I gotta stay loyal. Just because I got a career as a boxer, doesn't mean I'm any better than anybody. It doesn't mean I turn my back, and I don't turn anybody away. My door is open.

So my drug dealer friends start to ask if they can stash their stuff in my apartment because they know they can trust me. They know I don't do drugs. I'm not even drinking, not a drop. Everybody knows how I hate drugs. I'm a successful fighter. I'm not a drug dealer. I'm a safe bet and a good front. Pretty soon I got bricks of cocaine stashed up to the ceiling in my closet. And I don't think too much about it. I just go and look at that stash once in a while. And then I go out and train and win and go on with my life.

I didn't think that stuff can touch me. I didn't think, having stuff in the closet was going to make any difference. But there's an old Hispanic saying, "Live with wolves, and you learn to howl." Didn't take too long, before I start howling, too.

12

MY UNCLE RICHARD'S BODY WAS COVERED UP AND DOWN WITH SCARRED AND DIRTY TRACKS FROM NEEDLES, AND HE NEVER GOT BETTER, AND HE NEVER KICKED THE HABIT. He once saw me watching him shoot up, and his eyes were hollow, with dark circles, and his hands were shaking, and he said to me, "Don't ever try this, Johnny. Don't ever do it. Don't never be like me." I was little then, and I nodded. No way, Uncle Richard. Not me.

I was making the cover of magazines now. Top Rank had a million dollar Pepsi commercial on the table, being negotiated. I had sponsors and endorsements. I was the king of Albuquerque. Everywhere I went people wanted to talk to me, touch me, have my autograph. I had friends everywhere I went, instant friends. I was a big star, and I started to believe my own success.

But success is a drug in itself. And several hundred pounds of cocaine is a lot of cocaine to keep in your closet. I think back, it's amazing how long I held out.

I was high on my success. I went to more parties. I had more friends. I had more freedom. More attention. More money. More love. But I also still had a hole inside me that couldn't be filled.

And I started thinking about those bricks of cocaine in my closets. I started to tell myself how I deserved to have fun like everybody else. I started to think, maybe it's not so bad, maybe there's something to it.

I had stayed away from drugs for so long. I had hated them. Now, I started making excuses. Maybe I was being too hard on everybody else. Maybe a little cocaine wouldn't hurt anybody.

But I can't even say that that's where it all started. I had been around it my whole life. Everybody I knew did drugs.

My uncles used to make me sniff paint and glue when I was eight or nine years old. They'd spray it on a sock and make me inhale it and laugh when I fell down on the floor, confused and scared and disoriented. But from that time, I already knew what it felt like to lose yourself. To feel nothing in the power of a substance.

Or maybe it started with the beer my uncles made me drink before school in the morning, until I passed out or threw up all over the house and got my butt whipped by my grandpa.

Or maybe it started, watching the men who came to visit Claudio, tie their tourniquets in the bathroom. They taught me how to do it when my mother was out of the house, and Claudio was babysitting me. His friends whose hands were always shaking, and who told me to tie it real tight. I could tie a mean tourniquet by the age of six.

So part of drugs seemed normal, just part of life. I had resisted for so long. I started thinking that maybe it was me that wasn't normal.

I'm not trying to making excuses. I'm the one guiding my ship, me and the Good Lord above. But I took the wheel away from him that time. I won't pretend that it wasn't always all in my hands. I made my choices then.

Temptation.

You always gotta give something up, if you want to wear the devil's gold ring.

My Uncle Richard died. Died from blood poisoning. He came home one day with an infection in his arm that wouldn't heal. He lay around the house in a fever, moaning for a week. They finally took him to the hospital. The gangrene has spread to his heart. The doctors said he had to lose his arm to live. He refused. Refusing meant he was going to die. He knew what he was choosing. He died three days later.

I went to the funeral and saw my grandma crying because she lost her second child.

Her words were ringing in my ears, staring down into the grave of my uncle.

"Someday it could be you, and you could be worse."

Those words began to haunt me. Like she had spoken a curse and it was time to pay up.

The funeral. All that stuff about my mom had come back. How people die on you and disappear. Why am I here? What's it all for? Nothing matters anyway.

I opened those closets. I tried that cocaine. I didn't think it could do anything to me. But that was the fool talking. You know what they say: First time a mistake, second time a habit.

I loved the numbness. I loved how you could feel everything and nothing at the same time. It was made for me. And I never looked back.

I did drugs. I stopped drugs. I trained. I fought. I won, I went back to drugs. It took a while before anybody noticed. I had been clean for so long.

It was after the Gomez fight, my first USBA championship, my first big success, that the high was so high, the adrenaline pumping, and me feeling invincible. That's about the time when the drugs got bad.

And it was my success that tempted me, and it was the success that brought it all down.

Somebody makes an anonymous call from a party I was at, calling to the media, "Johnny Tapia, the boxer, uses cocaine."

Reporters show up outside my apartment, and they have to make it a big story. They don't know anything, but they print it anyway. They had me high for years, made me out to be the worst case in the history of boxing. Suddenly I can't go anywhere without people asking me about the drugs. "Is it true, Johnny?"

I can't face my family. I can't face the fans.

Something died for me then. Everything I worked so hard to build was all over, overnight. I had lost people's respect, and that's all I had ever wanted. People turned their backs on me. My family was ashamed of me. And worst of all, I lost respect for myself.

I fought Santiago Caballero in Albuquerque and I barely remember the fight.

They gave me three chances. I failed them all. It was already too late for me. Second or third chances didn't mean anything to me. Once it was done, I stopped caring.

I sat in front of the commission, in front of Stan Gallup, who now sat on the commission after the his Golden Gloves post, after having been one of my biggest supporters. I sat and listened to them tell me I was suspended indefinitely.

I saw tears in Stan's eyes. I know he hated suspending me. I know he couldn't understand how, after working so hard, after surviving so much, how I could throw it all away.

Paul convinces makes me go to rehab. He insists and I do it for him. But my heart's not in it and I take off after a month.

When I get back to my apartment to get my stuff, there's nothing left inside. I had debts and in the month I was gone people had come and taken everything. Everything I had. Even my USBA belt was gone. My car. My furniture. I had nothing left.

I called my family, called my grandpa but he is hard and proud.

"You're not welcome here no more, Johnny. You brought shame on the family. El que hace la paga. You made your bed. Go figure it out yourself."

They say there is no elevator to success. You have to take the stairs.

I had climbed those stairs, climbed every one. The thing they don't tell you is that if you miss a step, it's easier and faster going down than it ever was going up.

13

LIFE ON STREETS, HOMELESS, SLEEPING UNDER BRIDGES, ON PARK BENCHES, IN ALLEYWAYS, ON THE SCRUFF GRASS AT WELLS PARK COMMUNITY CENTER.

I went low. I went lower than low.

I'd stand outside my grandpa's house in the middle of the night, drunk or high, and just look. The lights would be out. I knew every tile on that linoleum floor. I longed for my place on the floor in the sun porch. But I never went in. Never even talked to them. I had brought so much bad publicity, bad shame, on the family. They had made it clear. They didn't want me. I was out for good.

I made it through for a while because I took out whatever money I had in the bank and spent it on drugs. Went from party to party, crashed on people's couches, slept in cars.

Every three days I'd come down enough to eat something. Stopped at a McDonalds and ate three Big Macs and three big fries. Then I'd go out again. Spend more money on drugs and party.

I stayed out of the daylight. Lived only at night. Didn't

Mi Vida Loca

want anyone to see my face. Didn't want anybody to see what happened to Johnny Tapia. Didn't call my old friends. Didn't talk to the Maloofs. Stayed away from everybody. I was so ashamed of myself, I kept myself numb and stoned. Did the drugs so I didn't have to feel anything.

If I had made it off the streets, now I was back. Back deeper and harder than ever before.

I did the parks where I knew they were dealing, I did the houses where I knew they were partying. I scored cocaine, drank beer, and got through another night. You'd be surprised how fast three years can go by like that and you don't even realize it.

The money ran out. Then I started stealing. I hooked up with guys who were doing jobs, and I broke into houses and stole what I could get to sell for more drugs.

It's the old story. Anything for drugs.

I got into plenty of street fights. If people hang out in the ghetto, eventually somebody's gonna start throwing punches. I was constantly beating up on anybody that was looking for trouble. And lots of people wanted a piece of me.

"Johnny Tapia. You think you're so tough, huh?"

"Johnny Tapia. Look at you now."

I'd have to beat on somebody, they start talking like that. Kept me sharp, at least. I guess I never really stopped boxing, even if it was just on the streets.

To feed myself, I jumped rope for people, just messing around, show them I could still do it. I can jump rope like nobody. Fast as hell, forwards, backwards, twisting, upside down, like a circus act. I'd draw a crowd and people would give me a couple dollars.

The Allsup's, where they knew me since I was a kid, stealing candy or running in scared from the alley for a doughnut for my uncle, they gave me a burrito once in a while if I came in real hungry.

The crazy thing is, no matter how low I had sunk, I was still Johnny Tapia, the Johnny Tapia. So people couldn't get enough with all my fuck ups. Everything I did, everyone ended up knowing about it. I'd get caught for burglary and end up in jail, and the papers would print it.

And I was in and out of jail constantly in those three years. They got to know me real well at the Bernalillo Court House. And every time I came out of that building, I'd have the reporters waiting for me there, shouting questions.

"You going to jail again, Johnny?"

But worst thing of all for me was how people I had known and trusted, for who I had done everything, anything they wanted, they had turned their backs on me. Partners I had, friends, didn't want nothing to do with me anymore. Didn't want me around. I had a reputation so bad, even the thugs didn't want nothing to do with me.

Go figure. They're out there committing some pretty bad crimes, but I was too low for them. Tells you something about how low I really was.

Only Randall was there for me then. I could go to him once in a while. We had always been the closest, and he still let me in. He had a little house and I'd crash there a few nights a week, and take a shower, and disappear again.

But Randall was always there. We're bonded to this day like that, I think because of living together like brothers, both of us living with my mother.

He had lost her in the same way I lost her. He was the one person who understood. We would talk about her. How we missed her.

One night, the lowest moment for me, I went to my mother's grave, flying high on speedball, and took a knife with me and cut myself up to kill myself. I wanted to die close to her. Right there on her grave.

But it was a strange thing, I cut myself and I was bleeding and losing consciousness, but then it was like an out of body experience. Like somebody lifted me and brought me to the park across the way, took me away from her grave. I still don't know how I got there. I still don't know what it was, but something saved me that night. And something turned around.

Three long years, three lost years.

I had won twenty three fights. I hadn't lost one. Some people would love to have that kind of record for their whole career. My career had barely begun and already ended.

Now I spent my time in and out of jail. But I wanted to box. I wanted to get back in that ring, that's all I could think of. I had to find a way.

I started fighting again for money. I fought in a bar called "Al Mi Gusto." They ran illegal bar fights every week in the beer cooler. These tough guys from Juarez would come up and wanna take somebody on. I'd fight anybody that came my way, for a pack of beer and three hundred dollars.

That was the beginning of my way back up.

And those fights were brutal, hard, down and dirty, bar fights, where anything goes. But I was undefeated as a professional. I sure as hell wasn't gonna lose some bar fight in some beer cooler.

The money kept me eating. The fighting got me into shape again.

One day Randall tells me Oliver wants to see me. He's got a job working for the city, running the Senior Center at the Barelas Community Center. He wants me to bring some pictures of myself, and sign some autographs for the seniors, and make like I'm a famous boxer.

Now, one thing you got to know about me, I have two favorite kinds of people. Children and the elderly. I love my elderly friends.

So I went to that Senior Center on pottery day. All these little old ladies were sitting at these long tables, making plates and vases out of slimy clay.

Oliver comes up kind of awkward, and he gives me a hug. Boy, had he changed. He had a wife and a kid, and a good steady job. He was the one who beat me the hardest when I was little, now here he was with the seniors. You just never know how people end up.

I came into that room with my voice booming through. I got a voice that I just can't keep quiet. It was great for the seniors, they all understood me.

Mi Vida Loca

"Hey, everybody. How are you doing today?"

They all nodded, grinning at me. I picked out one lady after another. There was Ida, Ethel, Mildred, Ruth, and Eileen.

"What's your name, sweetheart?"

"Mildred."

"Hello, Mildred. That's a nice dress you got on. You all dressed up today, huh?"

"Ida, your hair's so red. Where'd you get hair that red? What happened? You eat too much chili?"

I went from lady to lady, shaking hands, giving out autographed pictures.

"Johnny Tapia, professional boxer. What's your name, sweetheart?"

It was the most fun I had in a long time.

"Eileen. You got a husband? Well, you ever get rid of him, you give me a call, okay, sweetheart?"

I grabbed a few of them, the ones that could walk, the ones not on oxygen, and I made Oliver put on some Mexican music, and I made them all do some Spanish dancing.

I stopped at a special lady, real sweet and quiet, who's blushing when I sit next to her and ask her name.

She says it's Angelita, but they called her "Lala."

"Lala? Where'd you get a name like that? You like to sing, la la?"

She's blushing and giggling.

"You're a beautiful lady, huh? Would you give me a dance, Lala?"

I made her dance for three songs, twirled her all over the

room. By the end I had the whole room wanting to take me home and adopt me.

Outside the Senior Center, right across the street is Barelas Gym. My old place. I pointed outside for the ladies.

"You see that gym over there? That's my gym. I'm gonna be back in there someday soon. I'm gonna be fighting professional again. And I'm gonna send you all tickets and have you come and see me, okay?"

They all nodded.

"Until then I want you to pray for me, okay? Pray for me to be the best boxer in the world. I wanna be a world champion someday. Pray for me. God bless."

They all swore they'd put me in their prayers. I left that day feeling high on all that love and attention. I had missed that for so long.

That's what I got from boxing and I wanted it back.

But I was still screwed up. I went that night and did more drugs than I had in a week.

There was one more thing that had to happen to really bring me back again.

14

NEW MEXICO HAS THE HIGHEST RATE OF DEATH BY LIGHTNING STRIKE IN THE WHOLE COUNTRY. That's because you're out there in the middle of the desert and a thunderstorm can come up out of nowhere and you've got nowhere to hide. It could have been sunny all day, suddenly there's a huge cloud on the Sandia Mountains or on the Jemez Mountains, a huge thunderhead, and you're on a flat desert plateau, and you can try and run, but you sure can't hide.

Something like that happened to me in early 1993. I was struck by a kind of lightning, that I never saw coming. And it floored me, it leveled me good.

I was at a party one night, drinking some beers and talking with people, sitting on the kitchen counter, downing my plastic cup of keg beer, when the front door opens and in comes these two girls.

One of them I know. She's Ruth Montoya. I know her from around town. She went out with people I knew, and she was there looking for her boyfriend. She's got long, dark curly hair, and she laughs a lot and she's cute.

Mi Vida Loca

But the girl who was with her, I had never seen before, and she was a vision. She was incredible.

She stood there in the front door, just staying there, her arms held tight around herself, real quiet, looking kind of shy, but also like she had a lot of pride. She wasn't looking at anybody, just looking like she didn't want to be there.

So I hopped off the kitchen counter and walked over to her. She's not looking at me. On purpose. I stand in front of her. She still won't look at me.

"Hi, my name's Johnny Tapia. Professional boxer."

She finally looks me up and down, for a long beat, and she says, "Sounds like you got personal problems."

It hits my like a blow to my solar plexus. It was worse than some body shots I've taken in the ring. I could barely talk.

"What did you just say?"

"Look, I'm just waiting for my friend. I don't want to have a conversation."

People are laughing now, calling out, "Oooh, Johnny." I'm still trying to smile, still trying to be friendly, but it's getting harder. I hold up my empty cup.

"Want some beer while you're waiting?"

"Keg beer? I don't think so."

"What, it's not good enough for you?"

"You're not good enough for me."

People are really laughing now. I'm just stammering.

"You know, you gotta be the most unfriendly—," but she doesn't let me finish, finishes for me.

"--Bitch? So, what's your point?"

"I didn't say bitch. I wouldn't say bitch. That's not respectful."

She says, "Well, how about you respect my space and get outta my face?"

Ruth comes by and this girl grabs her by the arm and says, "Come on, I want to get outta here."

And that was it. Couldn't believe it, I was so mad. I went back in the kitchen, got myself another cup of beer and drank it, muttering to myself. I turned to the door, turned back, couldn't decide what to do, I'm so mad.

I never saw a girl like that. She was so beautiful, so soft and quiet, and so mean. And that pride. I grab a piece of paper from the counter and write Randall's phone number on the paper. Then I turned around again and ran for the door.

She's standing outside with Ruth and the two of them are laughing. I go up to her and she rolls her eyes, like I bother her, just looking at me.

I am looking at her, and I swear she was the most beautiful girl I had ever seen in my life. That long silky hair, those deep soulful eyes, her beautiful lips, and her beautiful figure. And that attitude. She was stunning.

I hold out the piece of paper and say, "I wanna see you again. Here's my number. Will you call me? "

She takes it in her hand. Looks at it. Then she holds it up and shreds it into little pieces and tosses it in my face, paper raining down on my feet.

"That's what I think of you."

Then she turns and she and Ruth go running off.

I'm standing in place, like my feet are in concrete, staring. I finally get my voice back.

"I don't care what you do!"

She keeps walking.

"You ain't gonna get rid of me!"

She keeps walking.

"I'm gonna marry you someday!"

She just keeps walking.

"Where are you going? Can I go with you?"

She's by the corner now.

"What's your name?!"

She's running off and gone.

I stood there like a fool. But I knew what I knew. And I meant what I said. She was the one for me. I knew from the moment I saw her. Now I just had to find out her name.

Being from the streets, I knew everybody. Knew all the families. Knew the turf. Knew the gangs.

Pretty soon I find out her name is Teresa. I know her cousins. Her brothers and sisters. And I knew I would find her again.

And I did. At the Burger King on Central. Found her with her cousin Ruth. Her eyes open real wide as she sees me coming, like she's thinking, "Oh, my god, there's that guy." I sat right down.

"Hi, Teresa. How are you? Why don't you ever call me? What's going on?"

She's trying not to smile. I take her hand and say, "You're

gonna be my wife. You just watch."

"Sure, sure, I'm gonna be your wife."

"You watch. I don't give up."

She rolls her eyes in this way that I know I'm always gonna like.

She takes her hand away and walks out.

If I make up my mind to do something, there's nothing to stop me. And if you try to tell me no, it just makes me want it more.

I go to her work. She works at "Titan Auto Insurance." I walk in one day and make a commotion until they let me go to her desk. The manager is trying to get me to leave.

"Sir, if you just come this way."

"I want some insurance!"

"Why don't you leave now?"

"No. I want insurance!"

I stand in front of her desk, pointing at her.

"From her."

She's turning red and tells the manager it's okay. When he leaves, she drops her voice.

"What are you doing here?"

"I want insurance. If anybody needs insurance, it's gotta be me."

"Oh, yeah? Why's that?"

"'Cause I was born on Friday the 13th. And that's pretty unlucky. There's gotta be insurance for that."

She looks at me with those eyes, kind of amused.

"There's no Friday the 13th insurance."

"No insurance for unlucky like me?"

"No. Not for unlucky."

"Well, I gotta have some luck. I'm standing here, talking to you and you're smiling... A little."

"I am not smiling." But she was.

I turn around and yell into the whole room.

"Hey everybody, I'm Johnny Tapia! Professional fighter! I want some insurance! This lady here says you don't have any for a guy like me!"

She pulls me outside and paces in front of me and she's real mad now.

"You're gonna get me fired."

"You? Fired? Who do I gotta beat up? Mr. Manager in there? Huh? Want me to rough him up?"

She looks at me, all upset.

"What do you want from me?"

"Go out with me."

"You're crazy."

"I wanna take you on a date."

"Why should I go on a date with you?"

"Because you're beautiful and I want you to be my wife. We gotta go out on at least one date before we get married."

She's looking away. I get an idea.

"I'll take you to a bar."

She looks at me, "I'm not twenty one."

"That's alright. I can get you in. This is my town. I can get you in anywhere."

I like to think she went out with me because of my charm

and my looks, but I think she thought I was weird and kind of amusing in some strange way, and she was up for an adventure. And I never failed in giving her that.

For a sheltered girl from California, "Al Mi Gusto" wasn't the kind of place Teresa had ever been to. She didn't grow up in the hood like me. She had grown up, watched over by a protective father who had recently died, and it forced her to move back with her mom in Albuquerque. She was so strong and so vulnerable and lost at the same time. And when she came into this bar she looked at everything and everyone like they were aliens from Mars.

It was Mexican night, so the ranchera music was playing all night, and everywhere you got these guys in cowboy hats and concha belts.

I get her set up with a couple of drinks and I tell her I'll be right back, since I had a fight in back and I needed the money for the date.

I come back twenty minutes later. I had put some guy into the floor who had me pretty good. He cut me in the face a few times, but I had him in the end.

So I come back to the table and she says, "What happened to your face?"

"Nothing."

Suddenly her brother, Robert, comes in and sees her sitting with me, and pulls her across the room, pulling her by the hand, looking mad. He's yelling at her across the room, "What are you doing with that guy? Are you crazy? Don't you know he's trouble?"

But that just makes her stubborn all of a sudden. She pulls away and she comes back to me, and she's a lot nicer, just to show her brother he can't tell her what to do.

"Where do we go next, Johnny?"

I take her by the hand with the case of beer under my arm, and three hundred dollars in my pocket, and I say, "Come on, let's get out of here."

We drive around Albuquerque in her car. We stop on the bridge and watch the lighting over the Sandias.

I take her to my grandparents' house where I introduce her to them. I say, "Grandma and Grandpa, I want you to meet my girlfriend, Teresa."

She rolls her eyes, but she smiles for them. They smile back and hand me a couple of trash bags full of stuff that they had kept for me for a while. They walk outside with us and they help put it in her car.

"Here you go, Johnny."

"Thanks, Grandma."

"Well, bye, Johnny. Bye, Teresa."

We get back in her car and she's confused.

"What are those bags?"

"Just some stuff they were keeping for me. Until I got my own place again."

"We're just on date. Where do they think you're going?"

"I guess they think I'm moving in with you."

She looks at me strange.

I just smile and say, "Hey, I'm hungry. Let's go to your house."

There are times, no matter how bad things can get, that I've just been flat out lucky.

That night, over at the little house on Foothill Boulevard and South Valley, was one of them.

Teresa brings me inside her mother's house, and here are two beautiful ladies sitting in the kitchen, her mom and her grandmother, making tamales.

Teresa'a grandmother, Angelita Mora, nearly falls out of her chair when I come inside because she's "Lala" from the senior's ceramics class, and she's acting like Elvis just walked into the room.

I sit down with them and introduce myself to her mom, Annie Gutierrez, and she instantly loves me, instantly loves me in a maternal way.

They set me to that table and I was doted over, cared for in a way that made my heart feel so good.

The whole thing is making Teresa pretty mad, frankly. She sits on the side, feeling ignored, while Annie and Lala are cooking for me, asking me a lot of questions. They want to know everything about my life. They cry for me when I tell them about my mother, about living on the streets, about losing my boxing license, about wanting to make good again. They laugh and smile when I tell them how I love Teresa and that I'm gonna marry her one day.

Hours go by and the clock on the wall says it's two in the morning.

Teresa starts to say that she's gotta get up in six hours and be at work and that she wants to take me somewhere. Annie and Lala jump in.

"But he's got nowhere to go. What's he supposed to do?"

Teresa offers to bring me to the nearest bridge, she's so mad right now, but Annie just wouldn't have it. So I see my opening. I turn to Annie all sincere, "Annie, since I'm gonna marry your daughter anyway, can I just live here?"

Teresa rolls her eyes.

"No, you cannot live here."

But Annie says, "Of course, you can, Johnny. Of course you can. You poor thing. You got nowhere to go."

Teresa looks at her mom, shocked.

"Mom, he can't live here!"

"Stop acting so paranoid, Teresa."

"Mom, I'm not paranoid. We don't even know, Johnny."

"Look at this boy. Look at all he's been through. He's like a son to me, Teresa. I can see his heart. This is a good boy. And he wants to marry you."

"Mom, this is crazy!"

I'm staying out of it.

"Johnny's got nowhere to go. He's got no one but us."

"Mom. He's made it this far without you."

"Johnny's staying. That's all there is to it."

"Oh, yeah? Where's he gonna stay?"

"In your room."

"Mom, in my room?!"

"Yes, in your room."

"Mom. We haven't even kissed!"

I try to smile at Teresa. She's steaming mad and she's beautiful when she's that mad.

Later that night, I'm lying in her bed. She's got nice pillows and a nice big fluffy comforter, and it's the nicest place I've slept for a long time. She comes in wearing all these thick clothes, sweat pants and thick socks, and she lies down on the other side of the bed and pulls the blanket over her head and won't talk to me.

I say, "Goodnight, sweetheart."

She says, "Don't you try anything."

I say, "Will you marry me, Teresa?"

"No."

Weeks go by like this. Teresa tries not to talk to me at all. Every day I ask her to marry me, and half the time she won't answer, other times she just says no.

She goes to work every morning and I go outside and wish her a nice day. She won't talk to me. I stand at the car, "Have a nice day, sweetheart." She ignores me.

I try to kiss her on the cheek, she rolls up the window and my lips catch on the glass before I can get to her. I stand in the street, yelling, "Teresa, will you marry me?" as she's diving off.

A couple of weeks later she gets sick and she's got a flu and a fever and she's feeling bad. I'm fluffing the pillows for her, making sure she's comfortable in living room. She's got the thermometer in her mouth. And she's beautiful even when she's sick. And she's frowning at me fussing over her,

"Stop acting like we're married, cause we're not."

But I get on my knee.

"Then marry me, Teresa. Be my wife."

From the kitchen Annie is yelling, "Marry him already, Teresa, I'm sick of hearing it."

"Mom. That's not how—"

I'm sitting at her feet, holding her hand.

"She's right, baby. You should marry me. We're living together. In sin."

She pulls back her hand.

"We didn't do nothin'. It's not sin!"

"Say yes, Teresa!" Lala is calling from the kitchen. "Just say yes!" Annie is yelling.

I'm looking into her eyes as sweet as I can.

"Just say yes."

Teresa looks at me, tired. She rolls her eyes.

"Oh, God. Whatever. I have the flu. I feel horrible. Just leave me alone."

I leap up with a hoot.

"She said yes!"

"I didn't say yes. I said whatever."

"She said yes!"

I go over to Annie and Lala and I'm hugging them. They're laughing and crying, and we're all hugging. Teresa is watching, shaking her head.

And suddenly all I can think is that I better make this a deal before she changes her mind. I got to get a ring, buy a wedding dress, book the hall. I run to the door.

"I love you, Teresa! I love you, baby! I'm gonna go now! I'll be back soon!"

And I'm running outside, and I don't even know why I'm running, except that I'm so happy, and I'm so high on this girl, and I'm just thinking, this is it, this is it, I'm getting married.

15

THERE'S A SAYING IN SPANISH: EMPEZAR LA CASA POR EL TEJADO. BUILDING THE HOUSE WITH THE ROOF FIRST.

If you don't have the foundation, things are gonna keep crashing down on you.

The Maloofs sponsored the wedding. Gave me money for the dress, the ring, the kegs and the liquor.

I bought the wedding dress in a shop on Central Avenue. It was me and a bunch of ladies giving me advice. I described Teresa. They pulled out a beautiful dress.

"Silk with pearl details, and lace on the arms."

I took the dress.

"You be good to her, hito."

"I will, Ma'am."

I showed up back at Teresa's house, with the wedding dress packed in a trash bag, and the Wells Park Community Center booked for Saturday.

It's Wednesday and Annie starts running through the house, "We're planning a wedding! We're planning a wedding!"

Teresa is looking at me, "Saturday?!"

We marry in the Wells Park Community Center. Teresa's still sick from her flu. Her whole family is there.

I'm standing outside on the sidewalk, with tears in my eyes, because from my family, hardly anyone was there. Fluffy, Berna, Anthony and Steven. All the closest ones to me didn't come. Not my grandma or grandpa.

Robert, Teresa's brother, stands next to me. Rob and me are close now. The family calls him "Gordy," but I call him "Robert G" and he calls me "J.T." I won him over, too. He's my best man.

But now I'm crying on the sidewalk and I won't go inside. The whole place is waiting on me. But I keep thinking they're still coming.

"Come on, man. Come inside, Johnny."

"Why wouldn't they come? Why wouldn't they come to my wedding?"

"Come on, Johnny, they're all waiting for you."

"It's my wedding, man! Why wouldn't they be here?"

He finally has to pull me in from the street.

We get married, and Annie's crying and Lala's crying, and Teresa's nearly fainting. I have to hold her up, her hands shaking when she says her vows. She looked so beautiful. But she looked scared, too.

And she was right to be scared. I had just run right over her. Never gave her a chance to think about what she was doing. But I've always been fast. Being faster than the next guy is how I win. It's my power.

I had piled on her with love so that she couldn't see the real me behind it. It was safer that way. I didn't want her to see the mess underneath. I made her life exciting and crazy, kept her off balance, kept her questioning. She was drawn in by my crazy charm, and pressured by her family. She didn't know how much trouble I was in. She didn't know she had married an addict. She was young and naïve, and sheltered. It's not that she wasn't smart. I just never let her know the truth.

There was a reception at Wells Park with cookies and punch. No alcohol because it was a Community Center. But I'm thinking, hell, this is my wedding, time for a party. So after twenty minutes, you know, a respectful amount of time, I turn to the room, and say, "Hey, everybody! There's a party at Annie's house! Everybody come to Annie's house!"

I had us hooked up with a keg, Coors Extra Gold, nothing but the best. I had put the word out on the street and pretty soon the whole house is kicking with people partying.

Annie didn't know she was throwing a house party. I made sure some buddies would show up with enough drugs to make it through my own wedding night.

To be honest, I barely remember the whole thing. I just know that pretty soon, things got out of hand.

Teresa is sitting in the living room by herself, feeling sick. People are getting drunk and partying all over the house.

Some argument gets started in the kitchen and I get in the middle of it. Pretty soon blows are being thrown and I get involved and the cops show up and are ready to haul me off, and the only reason they don't is because it is my wedding night, and Annie and Lala convince them to leave me alone.

The Maloofs had reserved us a room at the Sheraton Uptown, but I took Teresa to the "French Quarter Motel" on Central in West Mesa, a dive motel for hookers and their johns.

This is hard for me to admit. It's an ugly thing to look back on. And I don't remember any of that night from this point. I wasn't in my right mind. Wasn't in my mind at all. Wasn't thinking straight with all the substances inside me already. But I know I insisted on the "French Quarter" because it was close to party town.

I brought Teresa inside, put the bags down, grabbed her car keys and said I'd be right back. Then I got in the car and took off and left her there alone. I left my bride at the motel, never consummated the marriage that night, and ended up dead a few hours later.

The nuclear reactor I have inside, the crazy machine that drives me all the time, the manic energy that drives me beyond my best instincts and my best heart and my best wishes for other people, and for myself, it's like a machine that has possessed me. I could never stop an impulse. And I never knew why I did afterwards. Couldn't remember half the time. Just got some idea in my head and had to act on it. It's like the usual moment of judgment somebody has, just wasn't there.

Years later I would learn about my bi-polar disorder. Years

later I understood the chemical misfiring in the brain. But back then I was dousing my crazy fire cracker firing brain with so many illegal substances it just made for a cocktail of insanity.

My crazy life was inside of me, too.

I drove down South Central, found a house where I knew they were having a party. Somebody was doing speedballs and I got in on it. That's the last thing I remember before I died.

They found me dumped in front of a fire station in the South Valley. They brought me to BCMC University of New Mexico Hospital, registered as John Doe, DOA. Overdose.

It was some wedding night.

It was some honeymoon for my beautiful wife.

Teresa was woken up by Annie knocking on the door of the motel, "Teresa, come quick! It's Johnny! He's dead!"

They rushed to the hospital and were told I had been brought back from death, and that I might have such severe brain damage when I came to, they might have to make a hard decision about whether to keep me on life support.

Teresa had to face the fact that, less than twenty four hours after getting married, her husband was clinically dead.

The part I remember is waking up a few hours later in the hospital room, confused and panicked, seeing all the tubes and IV's sticking out of my arms.

I only had one thought, "I gotta get outta here."

You come out of a coma, you're bound to have crazy thoughts. All I could think is that if I didn't get out of there, somebody was gonna arrest me.

Teresa tries to stop me, Annie's pleads with me, while I'm ripping out the tubes and needles from my arms. Tore them right out.

I didn't bother with clothes. I run out of my ground floor room, and into the hallway, and before anybody could stop this crazy streaking man, I was already out into the parking lot, sprinting from car to car. I found Annie's car parked in back, found it unlocked, and jumped in and hid on the floor in the back seat. Stayed there for a long time, before Annie and Teresa came out.

I can see them peeking in through the window, shading their eyes from the sun, looking down at me, huddled on the floor in my hospital gown, waving for them to get in the car and get me out of there.

What could they do? They took me home and gave me chili. I laid down and slept for two days.

Right here and now I have to get something straight.

Teresa is a very, very smart woman and she always was. When I met her, she was always reading, and she still reads something like five books a week. She wanted to be a Russian Interpreter. She wanted to study archaeology and join the CIA and be a top-level agent, and work at high levels of government with access to top security level information. This is who she was before she met me. These were her dreams.

And I liked that about her. She was different.

You could argue whether it was all that smart to marry a guy like me. But once she made that mistake and said, "I do," she was smart at every step ever since.

She learned a few things, and some things took a while to come to light. But she understood quickly what she was dealing with. I was an addict. I was lost. I loved her with all my heart, but my heart had been booked by something else already, and it demanded all of me.

She tried for quite a while to help. She tried to watch me, play the cop with me, give me tough love, be patient, be understanding, be supportive, be wily, and be one step ahead of me. But in the end, it is a losing battle, until an addict is ready to get clean.

I loved her so much then. And I have always loved her. She looked like a beacon of hope. She shone something, a light in darkness for me. From the moment I saw her, she has been my woman, my angel, my mother, my friend, my protector, and my only one. I owe my life to her.

But she's had to go through a lot because of me. And she was so tough all along, and she made a lot happen for me and for us. I am indebted to her for the rest of my life. For my life, truly. For the fact that I am standing on this earth today, looking out at the trees and hearing the birds singing. There is only one person who is responsible for that. She gave me my life.

But for a long time, I couldn't be there for her. Even though she was always there for me.

Something I have always regretted.

It took her getting pregnant and having a miscarriage, and losing the baby while I was out on a two-week party binge, while she was all alone, for her to take real action. I was coming back wasted from drugs and drinking, ready to sleep for days, recover, eat, and disappear again, while she suffered alone. It was terrible for her. And she let me know just how terrible it was.

She said, "You clean up or we're done."

Foolish pride is the devil that fuels any addiction. So I went and partied as my answer.

She gave her mother the order, "I'm done with Johnny. He's got to move out."

Her mom said, "I'm not kicking Johnny out on the street. He needs help. He's sick."

"We're not gonna save him, Mom."

"He'll be alright. You'll see. We'll help him."

"We won't help him by constantly saving him from himself. He has to go, Mom. I want him to leave."

I told you, I had the mother wrapped up. And I love her deeply, but Annie was always taking my side, against Teresa.

"How can you say that? After all he's been through. How could you do that to him? Throw him out?"

"I'm serious, Mom. I want him out of this house!" Teresa told her.

Annie's a tough Hispanic Mama, and she'd rather die than abandon a sick child. In her eyes, Teresa was the healthy one. She didn't need the help.

She said, "Well... It's not your house, is it?"

Teresa couldn't believe it.

"What are you saying? You want me to move out?"

Annie just looks back at her, silent.

Teresa says, "You're telling me to leave?"

Annie just shrugs. "You do what you have to do."

Kicked her own daughter out of the house. But you know, Teresa didn't give in, didn't change her mind. Didn't beg and moan. Didn't backpedal.

She said, "Fine, if that's what you want. I'll move out."

Took her car. Took her stuff. Got her own little house to rent. Got a job. Paid her bills and wouldn't talk to me for nearly half a year. Wouldn't answer the phone if I called. Wouldn't open the door.

Her mom would call her and say, "Johnny misses you."

She'd say, "fine" and hang up.

I told you that girl is strong. Strongest woman I know.

So, now I'm living with Annie who dotes over me, cooks for me, makes all excuses for me, shows up at the night clubs and the bars, her hair in curlers, her nightgown fluttering in the wind, looking for me, bringing me home.

That woman played the role. I love Annie, and I always will. I called her "Mom" from the first day I met her. She might not have been helping me in the big sense, maybe not in the tough love department. But that wasn't her. She's old school, where Teresa is not. Annie was just there for me and took me in from the day I walked into her house. And I'll always love her for it.

But I was too much for Annie, too. Couple of months I'm

back in jail for violating probation.

So a year after getting married, I've been dead once already, my wife has moved out, and I'm living with her mother, and I end up in jail.

I died two more times in that same year. Once I met up with an ice pick in my head. Once more they found me dumped in front of St. Joseph's Hospital. DOA. Overdose.

I'm telling you, I've had more lives than a hard living cat.

I promised you, I had a crazy life. Find me one crazier than mine.

16

IN 1993, PAUL CHAVEZ WAS COUNTING THE DAYS UNTIL MY RELEASE FROM JAIL ON DECEMBER 23RD BECAUSE HE WANTED TO GET ME INTO THE RING AGAIN.

Teresa was counting her spare change at the end of every week of work, and counting the number of times I called her at home and the number of times she hung up on me when I did.

And me, I was counting the fingers on my hands, if I was sober or clear headed enough to make it all the way up to ten.

One day Paul Chavez shows up at Teresa's house and sits down in her kitchen.

"I think I can get Johnny to fight again when he gets out of jail."

Teresa said, "I don't want anything to do with him. I'm finished with him."

"But I think I can get his suspension revoked. You could take him back home with you and help him train."

"Why don't you take him home and train him?"

"Are you kidding? I'm scared of the guy. He could kill me

in my sleep."

"So, it's okay for me to get killed? Is that what you're saying?"

"Well, I don't know. You're married to the guy."

"Why do you wanna bother, Paul?"

"Because he's the best fighter I know. With your help, we can make sure he's clean and stays clean and get him back in the ring to fighting again. Teresa, he could be the best. He deserves that shot."

"But I'm not even talking to Johnny."

"Well, you're gonna have to talk to him."

Paul promises to pay her rent, pay her phone bill, and tells her she's gotta quit her job, and make it her job just to get me clean and get back into boxing.

My wife is a loving woman with a generous heart, but she's nobody's fool. She can be tough as nails, and she's the first one to know when to walk away from something.

But this was a challenge to her. It wasn't the CIA, and it wasn't living a Russian spy novel's life, but it might have come close. It tapped into all her smarts and wiliness.

I had hurt her so much, but she was willing to give this a chance, I think because she liked the challenge.

If there was ever any doubt about whether there are miracles in the world, the fact that she took me back in had to be the final proof. Paul still had to convince her pretty good, but she did finally agree.

She quits her job the next day. She has locks put on all the doors. She has wrought iron put on all the windows. She stocks the pantry up with food. And she answers the phone when I call. First time I talk to her in nearly half a year. I say I want to see her and she agrees to let me come over.

So I take a shower, rip some flowers from somebody's garden, and go knocking on her door. Little blue door on a little blue house.

She opens up, and I see her standing in the door, and she's all dolled up. And I swear she's the most gorgeous woman I ever saw.

"Hey, baby. I sure have missed you."

"Hey, Johnny," she smiles

"I'm so glad to see you, baby."

I walk in and give her the flowers, or the weeds, whatever you wanna call them. She's putting them away in a vase and I'm looking around the house.

"You made it nice, huh? It looks nice."

"Uh-huh."

"Did it all yourself."

"Uh-huh."

"It looks good. Looks nice."

She comes back to me, "Yeah, thanks." Then she locks three locks on the front door, takes the key, and throws it out the window.

I feel the panic in my gut right away. I don't like locked doors, I don't like being locked in. I look at her.

"What are you doing, Tree?" I always call her "Tree."

She shrugs kind of soft and simple, with a smile.

"It's just you and me now, Johnny. You're here to stay."

Then she goes and down sits in the only chair in the living room and picks up a magazine, all casual, and just starts to read, leafing through the pages, humming.

I start pacing in front of her. And I'm mad already.

"Gimme the key."

"Are you hungry, Johnny?"

"Give me the key, Teresa."

"There's food in the kitchen."

"Give me the key!"

"I can't. It's outside."

I'm furious.

"You gotta let me outta here!"

"No, I don't think so."

I pace back and forth, ready to cause trouble.

"You can't do this to me!"

But she just pages through the magazine, all calm.

"You let me outta here right now!"

She just keeps reading.

I grab a vase she's got on the mantle and throw it across the room where it breaks in a hundred little pieces. She just ignores me. I grab an ashtray and throw that, too.

She gets up and goes to a window, and takes the vase she's got put up with some flowers and hands it to me.

"You forgot this."

And I hurl it across the room and break that, too. Then she walks from the room and I go ahead and break every last piece of anything that's sitting free in that room. Broke everything in that house before it was all over.

"Teresa, I can't cold turkey this! I can't do that!" I told her.

She just said, "You can and you will."

And I did. A week of shaking, sweating, freezing, convulsing in agony, throwing up, and not sleeping at all.

Teresa would sit in the living room and read book after book and listen to me screaming in the bedroom, cursing her in between throwing up.

I would yell, "I hate you!"

And she'd yell back, "The feeling is mutual!"

It felt like it would never end.

But it did. After a week, I was clear enough to really feel my hate for Teresa. I paced in front of her, all day long.

"Let me out."

"No."

"I want out."

"No, Johnny."

You can't do this to me!"

"You're not leaving here, Johnny."

Annie would come and pass food through the bars in front of the door, feeding me like a dangerous animal. Pushing Sonic burgers through the bars. She'd beg Teresa.

"Teresa, can't I come in?"

"No, Mom."

"Why? Don't you trust me?"

"No, Mom, I don't."

And Teresa would shut the door again.

After the second week, I started getting my appetite back. I had lots of Snickers bars and Dr. Pepper, but also eggs in the morning and steak for dinner and burgers for lunch and it started making me feel strong again.

By the third week Teresa comes into the living room and sees me on the floor and I'm doing sit ups. I figure I might as well do something good. So I start working out. I do my sit ups. I do crunches. Push ups, side press, triceps, stretches. I start running in that little eight hundred square foot house, running in little circles counting hundreds to thousands of laps.

Teresa doesn't say anything. I can see her watching, but she doesn't want me to know. She watches from the kitchen and stays out of my way.

By the fourth week, Teresa starts looking real good to me. She just became more and even more beautiful by the day. I start to follow her around, in the kitchen, in the living room, back to the kitchen, to the bedroom. I'm saying, "You know, you're looking pretty good, Teresa." And she kinda of smiles, but she still pushes me away.

But by the end of that fourth week, I am so stone cold in love with her again, and probably more than I have ever been. Because I am clear headed and I am clean, and I can feel things again.

Also, it starts to get through my thick skull, and I do got a real thick skull, all from the boxing, that she's just done something really incredible for me.

One day, I go into the kitchen and I make her sit across from me and I take her hand in mine and I look into her eyes, really look.

"Thank you for what you've done, Teresa. Nobody's ever done anything like this for me before. Thank you."

"You're welcome."

"I feel better than I've felt in years. And it's because of you."

She says, "It's nice to see the real Johnny again."

And she smiles, "I may even learn to like you. Now that we're married."

I hold her hand in mine. I love her so much.

"I hope so. I sure hope so."

By the fifth week, the front door is opened for the time first. Paul Chavez comes over every morning and takes me running and training at the gym. I do a month of intensive training, and get back into shape. I'm feeling great and I'm ready. I can't tell you what it felt like to be back in the gym after almost four years. Four years of drugs and having been in jail and being a lost man on the planet.

I was ready to get back in the ring.

Paul has a fight set up. Jaime Olvera, in Tulsa, Oklahoma, a month away.

I got in the ring and knocked him out in four rounds.

Three weeks later I fight Arturo Estrada in Albuquerque at the Convention Center. You should have heard the crowd. It was my first fight back in a way. People are chanting "Johnny, Johnny, Johnny!" It felt so good to be home, to have the fans back behind me. I won by Technical Knockout in five rounds. I was clean and strong and fighting again. I never wanted it to stop.

And that's how Paul had it planned. Antonio Ruiz in Los Angeles, after that. Rafael Granillo. One fight after another, with only weeks in between, and right back to a fight again. He was keeping me focused, keeping me in shape, and keeping me out of trouble. And he was building up my record to show people I was really, truly back, and I was as good as ever.

I fought Oscar Aguilar in Phoenix and won the NABF belt with a technical knockout in three rounds. I couldn't be stopped anymore. I had to show the world, I was really a fighter and I was ready for a title fight. I was ready, truly ready for the first time, to become champion of the world.

I went to my grandpa's house one day to see him. I didn't tell them I was coming, but I go and stand at the door and knocked. The door opened and my grandpa sees me. He almost shuts the door. But I go up to hug him.

"Grandpa!"

He lets me hug him, but he's all stiff. I throw him some fake punches.

"How are you? You look good!"

"Run every day. Never miss a day." He pats his stomach, still proud.

"Still wear the clothes I wore as a young man."

"Yeah. You're in shape. You got that discipline, huh""

He nods and then he doesn't know what to say. But I'm excited to see him. I feel like I can make things right again.

"Hey, I'm fighting again, Grandpa."

"I heard that."

"You gonna come see me train?"

"Oh, you know. Paul don't want me around anyway."

"You come and see me."

"I'm not driving that much right now."

"Okay."

We're silent again.

"Hey, Grandpa. I'm going for a world title. You gonna come to the fight?"

When it came to my grandpa, my whole family, but especially my grandpa, I still felt like a kid, wanting to make him be proud of me.

"I don't know, Johnny. Sure. You know, maybe I'll be there."

I nod, awkward.

"You get those checks I send you?"

"Yeah-- We get 'em."

"Yeah? So. Well-- how's Grandma?"

"She's good. You know, she's the same. Her foot still bothers her. Same things."

"Yeah..."

This is hard for him and me.

"I miss you. I miss my family."

"Well, we don't hear from you. You're married now."

"Yeah, I was-- I was bad a while, you know? I was bad for three years, grandpa. But my wife, Teresa, she got me clean. You know, I'm better now, I'm back."

He just nods. Doesn't want to say anything.

"Hey, I wanted to come get my old trophies. You got my

old trophies."

Grandpa looks at me awkward.

"We threw them out."

I must've looked real bad, 'cause he even tried to make up for it.

"We needed the room, Johnny. You know? The rain ruined them. We didn't think you needed them no more. You know. The old junk."

I know he didn't mean it bad. But I gotta say it hurt. It really hurt.

"Yeah, old junk, huh? Junk. Yeah... Well, I better go."

He shrugs and nods, "Uh-huh."

"Tell Grandma I said 'hi'."

"Yeah. Okay."

"I'll be seeing you, okay?"

"Okay."

I turned and walked away and I could feel him watching me. I felt all kind of feelings. Happy and sad. Never easy for me to go back to that house, once I left. I walked across the street where I had seen my mother being dragged away by her murderers. And me and my grandpa probably both felt it, that bond that holds us together and keeps us apart.

17

WHEN THEY FOUND MY MOTHER SHE HAD TWENTY-SIX STAB WOUNDS IN HER BODY, STAB WOUNDS FROM A SCREWDRIVER AND A PAIR OF SCISSORS. She had been hit in the head with a hard object, like a crow bar or a wrench. She had been in and out of consciousness, left to die in a rock quarry on the outside of Albuquerque. She had crawled one and one half blocks out of the quarry and down the street, looking for help, crawled on her belly, her body torn up. A construction worked had found her on his way to work in the morning. He called 911, and she was rushed to the hospital.

She was registered in as a Jane Doe, and treated, while they waited for someone to come and claim her. She was alive for three more days. The police had little hope of solving the case and little interest, too. She was a Latina. A woman. And woman from a street culture, from a Hispanic ghetto culture that was known not to let the outside in.

In the hospital a nurse discovered mysterious head trauma that she believed to be new. But no one could explain it. And so no one did anything about it.

After three days the police decided to put her jewelry on the news hoping to identify her before she died and they would close the case. They got a call from an Ester Tapia claiming to be her mother. Her mother, father, and sister came to hospital and identified her as Virginia Tapia.

And then she died.

My mother had blue, blue eyes and long, black hair. Everyone said she looked like Priscilla Presley. Heads would turn when she walked by. In her life she projected beauty and joy and spirit and love. She drew people close to her just by being herself. Her heart had room for anyone that needed help, anyone that needed something. She loved life more than anyone else in her life.

And I had survived her.

I probably felt that burden every day. I had seen her taken away and didn't save her. I had known what happened and didn't stop it. She wanted to live. She called for help and I didn't help her. It should have been me. I shouldn't be alive, when she was dead.

Since then I have walked away from death so many times myself, I have outlived even the toughest, most indestructible cat around.

There were many times that I didn't ask for it, and I still survived. And there were also many times I did ask that death come for me, and release me from the pain and the guilt and the sorrow that I have felt every day of my life.

How can anyone live through such pain? How can any boy, see his mother be dragged off, taken away with brutality and murdered? How do you live on?

If there was one thought that drove me to seek to die as many times as I have in my life, if there was one thing that brought me to the brink of succeeding in dying so many times, it was this thought: "How can I be alive when she is not?"

Her death made me want to die.

Every day of my life I had that thought.

And yet there was another thought growing beside it.

A thought that kept growing and pounding on my skull. Who killed her? Who dared to take away my mother and make her suffer in such a horrible way? Who took my life away with hers? And how can I make him suffer like she did?

The drive for revenge was what kept me alive. It formed first when I began boxing. It fueled every match, every fight, every bout, every step into the ring, every time I would walk out, with my music playing and the crowd cheering me on, and the fans screaming my name.

But pretty soon all those sounds disappeared, and all thoughts and feelings disappeared, except the one thought that the man who was facing me in the ring, this was the man who killed my mother, and that killing this man would finally calm the rage I felt inside of my heart, every day of my life, that rage that had nowhere else to go.

In the ring I was calm. In the ring I felt that everything was alright. And that I would be alright. The ring is my peace. It has been a place of peace for me.

Only in the ring have I always truly felt right in my life. In

Mi Vida Loca

the ring, in the battle, in the one on one, in the contest which would leave the best man to remain standing at the end of the fight, that is the only place I really feel I belong. For me the battle is peace. For me the fight is my final and only rest.

Outside the ring, my heart, my soul, is troubled and restless. Inside the ring there is peace.

I fought Henry Martinez on October 10th, 1994. It had been nineteen years since my mother was murdered. It had been eighteen since I began boxing. I was twenty seven years old. I had been legally dead three times and escaped near death three times more. I had nearly ended my career with a near four year suspension. And I was back again. I was still alive. And I was finally fighting for the title of champion of the world.

The night of the fight, my dressing room was all craziness. All these people were coming in and wishing me good things. Beto Martinez is my cut man still, and he's wrapping my hands up. Paul is mad at all the people and wants to keep everybody out. He's pushing people out, slamming the door in people's faces.

I like to play music before a fight. I like to have a lot of noise and action around me. It pumps me up. But Paul wasn't having any of that. He was making Teresa stay out. Then it was time to get changed. A priest is there and he says a blessing for the fight. I kneel down, my people beside me, all of us blessed for the fight. And then it was show time. Time to go and fight for the title of champion of the world.

Ever since I had returned to boxing I played the song "My

Prerogative" by Bobby Brown, as the entrance song before the fight, just as I come walking up to the ring.

As soon as the music started up on this night, the University of New Mexico "Pit" arena went insane. "The Pit" was filled to every last seat, and every last person inside knew of what had happened to me in my life, both good and bad. They knew about the murder of my mother, they knew about my success, all my failings, my arrests, my drug suspension, my marriage, and my return to the ring to fight for my first world title ever.

When I came walking toward the ring, the whole place just went nuts. Everybody is chanting, "Johnny, Johnny, Johnny." Hands were reaching out for me, people were throwing me rosaries, throwing me crosses, telling me they were praying for me. The love from the crowd was overwhelming to me, and that love strengthened me in the ring and throughout the fight, the whole way through.

I had a new strength beside me now, too. My wife, Teresa. She stood by the corner, her beautiful, dark, serious eyes watching me, giving me strength.

And then there was something more. Something I didn't expect. My whole family came to that ring. They had bought their own tickets and never told me beforehand. My grandpa was there, and all my cousins, aunts and uncles. Everyone except my Grandma Ester. She said she would rather stay home and pray for me. But I was surrounded by the rest of all my family, and it made the whole experience so much more emotional, from beginning to end.

Mi Vida Loca

Henry Martinez was a good fighter. I had to work for every moment of that fight. But I was just too fast for him. I had him off his game the whole time.

I stayed focused round after round. Paul is behind me, talking in on me, but I knew in my heart, there was no way I was not gonna win this one.

The crowd was behind me and it gave me strength. I fought focused, round for round. Every time the bell rang I charged into the ring and Paul is yelling for me to slow down and get my footing. But I couldn't wait to get back in there. I was on it. I could taste the win.

In the 11th round I knocked Martinez off his feet so hard, I got the technical knockout. The referee ended the fight, and suddenly it was all over.

When they announced that I won, I dropped down to my knees. I felt my legs give in, as they were saying I was the new champion of the world, and the strength left my body and I dropped down, humbled and grateful. Tears were streaming down my face. I looked up to the heavens, up to my mother, and I made the sign of the cross over me. I cried and thanked the Lord Almighty, and I told my mother how much I loved her and that I hoped she was proud of me. I told her how much I missed her, that I wished she could have been here to be with me and see me win the world championship, to win it just for her.

Everyone in the arena was on their feet, everyone crying, I swear, not a dry eye in the place. I was crying and everyone in that place was crying with me. I will never forget it for my whole life.

I got up off my knees finally and got up and again and turned to the crowd. They were screaming and roaring and chanting, "Johnny, Johnny, Johnny."

Finally I could feel all the joy flow through me and I ran across the ring and jumped into the air. I jumped in the air with the joy of winning and the joy of reaching my dream. And I threw my body into a full turn in the air and flipped head over heels and landed back on my feet. The crowd went crazy for it.

It became my trademark. All the days on the trampoline at Wells Park. Just a bonus for the fans.

I kissed Henry Martinez on the head and hugged him. I told him he's a good man and he was a generous fighter. He congratulated me.

I grabbed Teresa over the ropes and kissed her. I yelled to my grandpa who was standing, waving to me. I yelled for him to come up and come inside the ring. He climbed through the ropes and I lifted him off his feet and carried him around the ring.

It was an amazing night. It was everything to me. Everything, all the years, all the fighting, it all came together. I can't tell you with enough words how much it all meant. It was so special.

The end of a long time of fighting. And the beginning of a new time to come.

18

Ya que estamos en el baile, bailemos.
Since we are at the ball, we dance.

I WISH I COULD TELL YOU THAT EVERYTHING WAS GREAT AFTER THAT VICTORY. I wish I could have just taken that victory home in my heart and let it give me peace for the rest of my days. But peace never came to me easy. And when it came, it never stayed for very long.

The night and the day after a fight, the days and weeks after a fight, they are the worst of all the times I have in life. All the excitement, the anticipation, the battle and the victory, are all over. All the love, the attention, the adrenaline, the fans, are all gone.

After the high, and it's always the greatest high for me, I go low. I go real low after every fight.

You wake the next morning and you're pissing blood. Every part of your body aches. Your eyes are swollen, your face is bloodied, the bones in your hands are broken.

I don't go around crying. That part is part of the deal.

It's the silence. And the letdown. It's the fact that it's over.

Mi Vida Loca

It's just hit a low that makes me restless and moody. I feel trapped all of a sudden. The training is over, the focus is ended, and all my demons are calling me.

I held it pretty well together for a long while. It meant a lot to me to be world champion. I put the belt up on our television. We had bought a new trailer, our own trailer in West Mesa with some of the money from the purses in the last year. We had our own home with furniture and a big screen television. A television that I never watched, because I can't stand to sit down. Or if I watched it, I'd do it standing up. Standing or pacing. Pacing and pacing, watching the news or a Friday night fight. Most things people do sitting down, I do standing up. That's always the restless thing in me.

The championship put me in a whole new league. I was a defending champion now. I had plenty of fights ahead, and I trained and worked hard for all of them.

Paul Chavez didn't let me take any time off.

Two months after the Martinez fight, I knocked out Rolando Bohol in two rounds in Albuquerque. The fans were back again, supporting me, their hometown champion. I had put their city on the map. They shared that pride with me. I brought a lot of attention to Albuquerque, and the fans never forgot it.

You go through a hard time and people see you overcome, and they want to support you. Fans have always been there for me like that. Because I think they know that I know I'm just like them. I'm no different than anybody else. I'm a human being with two hands and two feet like the rest. We all struggle, and if I can come back from all the bad things that happened to me, and I can become world champion after all that, then anybody can make it in this world.

If I can give just one person hope with my story, then that makes it all worth it for me.

I fought Jose Sosa and successfully defended my title in Albuquerque. I fought Ricardo Vargas and defended my title in Las Vegas.

Every two months Paul Chavez and Top Rank promoters had something new for me to do, and I went out and got the job done.

I was still undefeated. And I couldn't be stopped. Paul was now looking for another title fight. Looking for me to win the IBF championship. And that championship had just been won by another fighter from Albuquerque, New Mexico, a young guy named Danny Romero, who they called "Kid Dynamite." And a rumbling began that would grow into a whole new kind of turf war. The fight for Albuquerque.

After I won the WBO title against Martinez, and Danny Romero won the IBF title against Francisco Tejedor, people started wanting to see us two as the competing Albuquerque champions. It was something promoters and public relations people could really run with. It became a war over popularity. A war over turf. I was turning thirty and he was only twenty three. He was just coming up, and being heavily promoted. Promoted on his good, and my bad, reputation. But it took many more years and a lot of press before it came to a showdown.

While all this was brewing, my demons had a full chokehold on me again. I had stayed clean for a long time, a long time after fighting again, but after the Martinez win, and all the big press, and the pressure, and the new power making me drunk, I fell back into the old ways, and without Teresa knowing it, I started with the drugs again.

There was just too much to party about, too much attention, too many people wanting to hang with me, wanting to seduce me back into that life.

Often people would come to me and press a packet of cocaine into my hand secretly. All the time I was trying to stay straight, people would slip me drugs and I had to throw them out.

Drugs were the only way to get close to me. Straight and clean, I like to hang out at home alone with my wife and I'm happy like that. But when I'm high, I wanna be out there among the people, people doing the same crazy things as me. Drugs had me on a leash when I was hooked. Give me drugs and people knew they could be my best friend. Addicts are easy. And I think these people thought they were doing me a favor.

I had stayed clean for seven or eight months. Maybe I had managed it just that long. But suddenly I was deep in trouble again.

I started doing so much cocaine that I became a complete paranoid. I kept thinking the police were just outside the trailer where we lived. I had Teresa climb trees, looking for stakeout cars. This is a girl who doesn't like to break a nail, or a sweat, and she's climbing up these trees because I got her convinced the FBI is staking me out.

She kept saying, "I don't see anything, Johnny."

I keep saying, "No, look harder. I can see them. They're out there. They're after me."

I had her hide me in the closets, put blankets on my head in case they tried to look for me.

I had Teresa convinced. I think she really wanted to believe, because any other explanation would be worse. She didn't want to see what was really happening.

I wouldn't let her turn on the TV at night because they would see I was home. I made her keep the curtains shut. I wouldn't let her use the phone.

She finally called Randall and told him how concerned she was about me, how the police were after me. He laughed. He said, "Teresa, he's high." She said, "No, Randall. It's the police. They're after him." He said, "No, Teresa. He's high. This is the kind of stuff you make up in your head when you're high."

I know it must have hurt Teresa when she found out. I know she knew it was true the moment he said it.

She doesn't tell me what she knows. Instead, she hides me in the closets and puts the blankets on my head and leaves me there. And when I say, "Can you see them, Tree? Are they there?" she says "Yes. They're there. You better stay there for a long time. I can see them right outside." And she'd leave me there for hours, sometimes the whole night. Every time I asked, she said they were still there. At least she got a little bit of revenge.

Then she confronted me.

"I know you're high."

"No, I'm not."

"Yes, you are. Don't lie to me."

She called Paul Chavez. They both made me go into rehab in Las Cruces. I was there for three weeks. There were more drugs on the inside than there were on the outside.

Teresa calls me and notices that I am totally high. So tells me it's time to come home. I refuse to leave.

She calls me back and tells me some story about a judge being on his way to the rehab where I was to drug test me right there and that I had to leave.

She hijacked my butt right out of rehab just to get me clean. Unfortunately, that's how rehab goes sometimes.

No matter what she did then, no matter how smart she got, it was too late to save me. I was too far gone. I was ready to destroy myself and everything around me. Again.

I wasn't listening to Teresa. I wasn't listening to Paul Chavez. I was rebelling against his strict control of me and I was resenting the hold she had on my life. I stomped out on training. I ditched Teresa in restaurants, lied to her about where I was, staged false phone calls, saying I was home and training when I was out partying. I took off with all our money, and made her walk home. I was gone for weeks and she had to keep up the good face to the outside.

I would go off for weeks, and not remember what I did. I might wake up on some Indian reservation, on Acoma or Sky City or Laguna. I'd barely remember dancing around a fire, a headdress on, the guys pounding on the drums in their pow-wow, me whooping and dancing and drinking and falling down laughing. I might take a joy ride to Mexico with some compadres in a big junker car, and play the big time boxer in the clubs in Juarez, where they loved me so much, or party at a week long underground fiesta, or I might end up in a drug dealer's hideout deep in the hood, face down in cocaine.

Sometimes she'd call Randall and they'd get in the car and go look for me. Sometimes they'd find me. Usually not. And then she'd have to stay at home and just wait for me to return. She had to call everybody. She had to tell Paul everything is alright. She had to call Bruce Trampler, my matchmaker with Top Rank, and keep things on track. She had to call Stan Gallup. Beto Martinez. She had to cover for me all the time, with people wanting to speak to me, with the papers asking questions. She held it all together. It was a bad, bad time for her.

But we were both in the dance. And since we were at the ball, we danced the dance.

No matter how smart she was, no matter how free her spirit, no matter how much power she had inside, she was forced to keep up our public life, along with propping me up all the time. She couldn't just move on, or just move out, even though she probably wished she could many times.

I'd come home after weeks, nearly dead and get back into training. I'd train and win a fight and disappear again. I'd soak up all the love of the crowd, my arms raised in the ring, and then I'd go home and crash deep into darkness, a darkness I can barely describe. Pain and emptiness and depression. And that's when the call of the addiction would come right back on me. The weeks and months of being clean all over in a night. I would disappear for weeks again. Teresa at home alone, not knowing if I was dead or alive. Not knowing if I would ever come back.

Things got so bad, we barely spoke to each other. Or she didn't speak to me whenever I came home.

Then Paul had scheduled a press conference to announce the Arthur Johnson fight. I was supposed to be there at ten in the morning. But I hadn't come home in weeks. I show up in the middle of the night I don't know how I got there. I just remember walking up to the house, and the door being locked, so I start yelling.

"Teresa, open up!"

I can see the car in the driveway.

"Come on, Teresa. Open up!"

I'm pounding the door with my fists.

"Open the fucking door!"

She won't come to the door. So I took the door off the hinges and went inside. Teresa's coming in from the bedroom. She can see I'm out of my mind.

Teresa walks right past me, mad.

"I'm leaving."

I go after her.

"Where are you going?"

"I'm leaving!"

I grab her arm.

"You can't leave me!"

"Let go of me, Johnny!"

I let her go. I can't believe it. And I'm out of my mind. I'm not thinking straight. I pull the .38 I was packing at the time.

I always had a gun. Everyone has a gun in the ghetto. Ever since I was a kid I was around guns. My grandpa's whole family was armed. Armed and dangerous. And I was, too, in that moment.

I point the gun at her. I can't tell you what I was thinking. I wasn't thinking. I was crazy, scared, and high. I was seeing things. Hallucinating.

"You can't leave me!"

She faces me, and she looks so proud and angry.

"Go ahead. Shoot me. I don't care. Just make it quick."

"I'm gonna do it."

"Fine. Dead or alive. At least I'm away from you."

I'm shaking now and she can see it. She tries to calm me down.

"Johnny. Why don't you go inside so the neighbors can't see you?"

"I don't wanna go inside!"

She's holding her cell phone in her hand.

"If you don't stop, I have to call police." I just got more crazy.

"Police?!"

All I can feel is the blow of that word. The betrayal. You just don't use that word in the ghetto.

"You wanna call police?!"

I drop the gun and grab her phone and dial 911 and hand it back to her.

"There. Call police!"

She hangs up the phone, "No, Johnny."

"Come on, call police! Tell them who I am! Tell them I'm Johnny Tapia! Go ahead! Tell them!"

She looks at me like she feels sorry for me. She picks up the gun and empties out the bullets. That's when I hear sirens and I take off running.

I run through several of the neighbor's yards, and hide in a shed in somebody's driveway, and wait for the sirens to pass.

Then I creep back 'cause I wanna see what's going on. I pull myself underneath a pick up truck across the street and let the oil out of the transmission and the engine, and then I cover myself with it. Cover myself with oil so the K-9 dogs can't find me. Funny how you can think some pretty smart things when you're stupid and crazy.

That's how I spent the rest of the morning. The sun is coming up. I'm hiding under the neighbor's pick up truck, smeared full of transmission fluid and motor oil. I'm waiting and watching, high out of my mind, paranoid, delusional. And slowly feeling pretty stupid, hanging there under that car, smeared full of engine grease.

I can see the police cars come and go. Police are talking to Teresa and then leaving again. I can see her inside the trailer window, talking on the phone.

Then I get a really brilliant idea in my head. When you're delirious on drugs, you think every thought you have is brilliant. I decide I could just go inside that trailer and tell Teresa that I have been working out and she's bound to believe me.

I get out from under the car and go to the door. I knock on the door, I'm convinced she'll believe me. I've already forgotten everything that happened before.

She opens and looks at me, covered in motor oil.

I say, "Hey, babe. I just ran four miles. I've been training real hard."

She studies my face for a minute, confused. Then she smiles, like you do when you humor a crazy person.

"Sure, Johnny, that's good. Why don't you come inside?"

She lets me in. I go and sit on the couch, because I'm tired all of a sudden. I've convinced myself by now that I really have just been running four miles, so I figure I must be winded. I lay back and I'm just happy to be home. I've forgotten the gun. I've forgotten the weeks I've been gone. I'm convinced I'm in training.

Then I start to see a room full of people, friends coming inside. Teresa watches me as I start handing jackets to people that aren't there.

That's about when the reporters come and knock on the door. Teresa says, "Don't open it!" but I open it anyway.

I let them in and make them sit. I sit down and they start asking me questions about the police incident. They see that I'm hallucinating. Teresa tries to get them to leave but they won't. She goes to call our lawyer while I'm sitting and talking to them and I'm petting a dog beside me that isn't there. I introduce them to my friends in the room, and I don't under-

Mi Vida Loca

stand their curious faces. But they seem to like listening to me, so, I keep talking.

Jerry Wall, our attorney, finally shows up and gets them out of the house. It's nine o'clock. The press conference is at ten thirty.

Teresa tells me we have to leave, but I tell her I can't do it. "Johnny, you have to."

The phone rings. She makes me take the phone. It's Bruce Trampler from Top Rank.

I tell him, "Bruce, I can't make it, man. I can't do it. I can't go."

Bruce says I have to.

I offer him fifty bucks if he does it for me.

I hear him laugh on the other line.

He says, "Okay, Johnny, I'll do it," he says, "for fifty bucks. You owe me."

Bruce is a good guy, and always was a good friend. As my matchmaker he's always had to make everything work. He's a serious guy, kind of shy, quiet and real smart. But he always cares a lot. He always really took care of me. We still talk together and work together if you can believe it. Once in a while he reminds me that I still owe him that fifty dollars. I guess I still do.

While the press conference is happening, Paul comes over and smuggles me out of the house and out of the media spotlight and takes me to Las Vegas to train for the Arthur Johnson fight.

And I got it together, once again.

The Johnson fight was big. A hundred thousand dollar pay day. A year before that fight I was homeless, sleeping in cars.

I won that fight in twelve rounds. It's still hard to see how I kept the record I have. With all the problems, all those years I was a real mess, I still was undefeated. I stayed undefeated for eleven years straight. Maybe that's why everybody put up with me for so long.

19

AFTER THE ARTHUR JOHNSON FIGHT WE MOVED INTO A NICE NEW TOWNHOUSE IN THE NORTH VALLEY, OUR THIRD MOVE IN ONE YEAR. The purses were growing and moving took our minds off what was really going wrong in our lives.

It was Sunday night. We had just moved in the day before. Ten days later, on a Monday, I was scheduled to appear in court for pulling a gun on my wife. I was looking at time in federal prison. It was not looking good for me. There was only one way I knew how to deal with trouble. Our first night in the new townhouse, I disappeared again and took off with the purse from the Arthur Johnson fight, a sixty six thousand dollar check.

Teresa doesn't hear from again until I turn up DOA at Presbyterian Hospital, registered as Sierra Doe. They tell her to come and identify the body. I pull out of DOA and come back to this world, pull out the tubes from my body and take off. I go home, sleep, and when Teresa turns her back, I leave and I'm gone again.

I had some partners who ran a drug dealing operation out

of a chop shop business front in South Valley. I could hide out in that place for weeks and spend most of my purses on cocaine.

It was from there that somebody called my wife and tipped her off to where to find me and what I was up to.

So this time she knew where I was. And this time she had a plan.

There are things about my wife I can't say enough. She is the strongest and smartest woman I have ever met. She has the inner strength of ten people, and maybe that's why she tried so much to deal with me instead of giving up, instead of walking away, like she could have so many times.

She also loves a challenge. So when it comes to having to be really smart, to put those FBI, high level security instincts in her to use, that's when she really kicks in. This time she had me. She really had me good.

It's two thirty in the morning. I'm having a high old time in this warehouse drug den where the music's too loud, and I'm yelling too loud, when somebody says, "You better hide. Your wife is here."

I ran and hid in the mechanic's pit of the chop shop underneath the gut of a car and watched the front door.

I was expecting an angry Teresa to be standing at the door, browbeating the bodyguards into telling her where I was.

But, no. Instead she was standing at the door with a couple of beer coolers in her hand and her cousin Ruth by her side, and she's all dolled up. They both got their jewelry on and their hair up in curls, their make up shining. They looked like they were ready to party.

I was thinking, "What the hell is this?"

You gotta know, as long as I've known Teresa, other than on that first date we had, my wife does not party. She does not drink. She does not do any of the crazy things that I have. And here she was, twinkling her beautiful eyes, tossing her long hair. I was freaking out.

The guys let the girls inside right away. They sit them down and a bunch of guys are sitting around them right away. They're smiling and laughing with them. The guys offer them coke and they just giggle and shake their heads and sip on their wine coolers in a flirty way.

Frankly, that's all I could take. I came crawling out of that pit, charging out from under that car, running right up to her.

"What the hell are you doing here, Teresa?!"

She's acting all innocent.

"What?! Me and Ruth wanna party."

I take her hand.

"You're coming with me."

She pulls away.

"I don't wanna leave."

"You're coming home with me right now!"

"Leave me alone, Johnny. Let me have some fun."

She made me so mad, I grabbed her by the arm and dragged her outside, Ruth following. Teresa's complaining that I'm ruining her good time. Ruth is mad that she doesn't get to party. I was so furious with both of them, I didn't snap to what was going on.

Teresa's pouting all the way back to the townhouse.

I keep saying, "What the hell were you thinking, Teresa? You're my wife! You can't just go out and party in some place like that! Those guys are drug dealers!"

She just rolls her eyes.

"You're just no fun, Johnny. You never let me have any fun."

We get back to the townhouse and we go inside.

It's dark in house and just as soon as she closes the door behind me, I get this bad feeling. I catch an image in the darkness, in the corner of my eye. Is that Annie in the kitchen? Isn't that Robert in the living room? What are all these people doing here?

Next thing I know, I'm looking at this serious dude, who's a doctor, and he's ramming a needle into my arm, telling me to relax. They're all holding me down, and I try to fight them all off. But then the world goes black.

Teresa planned the whole thing. The doctor keeps me sedated until Monday morning, when I've got to be in court. I barely remember standing before Judge Frank Allen.

And Judge Allen was good man. He knew me from all the years in court and from my boxing, too. Had seen me fight in the ring, and had seen me a few times too many in his courtroom as well.

Through the blur of my half waking sedation, he looked really fed up with me that day. I couldn't barely speak, my tongue heavy in my mouth, my brain all foggy. I kept thinking, "This is bad. I'm going down. It's prison time for me."

But Teresa had worked it all out. Our lawyer had talked to the judge and to the D.A. And my wife stood before that judge, and she said, "Judge Allen. I know you know Johnny. And I know you know he's a good person. He's not a criminal. He's an addict. He's sick and he needs help. He needs treatment, not prison time."

That woman. There is no better woman.

Judge Allen said, "Alright, Teresa. I will allow for probation only. But he'll have to leave the state for eighteen months. I want him to enter outpatient intensive treatment, attend anger management classes, submit to random drug testing, and visit his probation officer once a week. I don't want to see him in New Mexico for eighteen months. Make him stay away, stay clean, and stay out of my courtroom. Next time, he's going away for good."

I swear, Judge Allen saved my life that day. If I hadn't been all drugged up and woozy, I would have kissed him right there in the courtroom. I could still kiss him today. My wife made it possible. And he saved my life.

Before I could say "thank you," before the gavel could hit the judge's desk, the good doctor shot me up with some more sedatives, enough for everybody to throw me in the car and drive me straight out of the state.

It was the first time I ever left New Mexico to move somewhere else. I wasn't looking out at the sights. I wasn't talking about how things were going to be when we got there. I didn't stop at any souvenir shops in Gallup. I didn't take a side route through the Grand Canyon.

No. I was out cold. Teresa's sitting next to me, watching my breathing, while her brother Rob drove the van, without stopping, all the way to California.

Next thing I know, I wake up, sleeping next to my wife in bed. It's pitch dark. I jolt up and have a strange feeling. I get up out of bed and think, I better go and get a glass of water. I leave the bedroom and head down the hallway to the kitchen, but suddenly I'm falling down a set of stairs I never knew existed.

I fell head over heels, fell all the way down to the bottom, bouncing down the steps, landing flat on my back, staring up at a frightening sight. In front of me there are some sliding glass doors and outside those doors there are trees. Big, old motherfucking trees. Pine trees, too.

I rub my eyes. I shake my head. I blink. All I see is trees. So, I start yelling, panicking.

"Teresa! Teresa! I'm having a bad trip and I can't wake up! Teresa! You gotta come! I can't wake up!"

I go to the sliding glass doors, my hands in front of me like a blind man. When my fingers touch the glass, it feels cold and freaks me out even more.

"Teresa!"

I get a hold of a handle and rip the doors open and step outside. The smell of pine hits me in the face. There's pine needles sticking in my bare feet, and all I can see is the forest. Scariest thing I ever saw.

"Teresa! I took something awful! I can't wake up! I'm seeing things that aren't there! Teresa, come quick!"

The Crazy Life of Johnny Tapia

Teresa comes running down the stairs. Running up to me now. I'm running around like a chicken without a head.

She's grabbing my face saying, "Johnny! Johnny! Calm down! Calm down!"

"No, you don't understand! All I see is trees! Oh, my God! I'm tripping! What did they give me?"

"Calm down, Johnny! It's okay!"

I grab her hand, putting it on my chest, "Feel my heart! Is it beating too fast?"

"It's okay! You're okay! You're not hallucinating!"

"They slipped some acid! I don't do that shit! They finally slipped me some acid! What am I gonna do?!"

"Listen to me, Johnny. Listen to me. Listen to me."

I finally stop and look at her.

"Okay."

She looks at me serious.

"We're in California. We're in Big Bear. You're not dreaming."

At first it doesn't make sense. Slowly the words hit my brain. I calm down. I look at her.

"What do you mean?"

"We don't live in Albuquerque anymore."

I'm starting to feel sick feeling in my stomach.

"Teresa? What did you do?"

"We live here now, Johnny."

I look at her. Or maybe the word is "stare." I stare at her a long time. She's looking a little nervous.

"Johnny. I had to do it. We didn't have a choice."

Mi Vida Loca

I don't say another word. I turned around, walked back up those damn stairs and slammed the door.

She moved my ass out of New Mexico without asking me. Without telling me.

I was mad for a month.

Rob, Teresa's brother, is now my full time helper in the gym, and has moved out with us to Big Bear. He's helping out with training every day and he gets so tired of me ignoring everybody, he finally lets me have it good.

We're at a 7-Eleven store and we're both getting food and he's standing at the hot dogs and he asks me if I want one, and I'm just ignoring him like I had been for weeks for being part of my kidnapping to Big Bear. So he finally blows up at me, pointing at me with this hot dog wiggling in his hand, pointing it at me like a finger.

"Man, Johnny, ever since we came here, nobody can talk to you, man!"

I said, "You came. I was kidnapped."

He said, "Johnny. You were out of your mind. You were on your way to prison for good. Teresa saved your sorry ass."

I just turned away.

"Whatever."

"Yeah, whatever. Forget it. You're just full of yourself. Don't think of anybody else."

I turn away. Suddenly I feel this hot dog hit the back of my neck. I turn around all mad.

I'm looking at him, threatening.

"Did you just throw a hot dog at me?"

"Johnny. You promised me. When you married my sister, you promised me that you would never hurt her! You remember that, Johnny?"

"Did you just throw a hot dog at me?!"

"Where the fuck were you every time she was alone, thinking you were dead, huh? You sure as hell weren't there! I was!"

He's steaming mad, but all I can think of is this hot dog on my neck.

"Well, okay, Rob, but I'm not the one throwing hot dogs, man."

"Yeah? Well, I was there! Yeah? I held her hand, man! And you promised me you wouldn't hurt her!"

"Yeah? And you made me a promise, too! You would beat the shit out of me if I did. Remember that, tough guy? Why don't you keep your promise?"

"Damn straight, I will keep my promise."

At this point I grab a hot dog.

"Then come and get it, man!"

Rob comes charging at me. I throw the first hot dog. He grabs a handful and throws a bunch back at me. I grab some more and hold them up in my hand, showing them to him.

"Come on, Robert G. Don't make me do this."

Rob hauls to punch me but I rain a bunch of hot dogs, back on him.

The whole thing ends up in an ugly scene. The owner of the store comes up, waving his hands. We're throwing hot dogs at each other cursing each other.

Finally he hits me right in the eye and I turn away, doubled over, holding my eye.

Rob quickly comes up to me, concerned.

"Johnny! Johnny? You okay?"

I'm still holding my eye, moaning.

"Johnny?"

"Jesus, Rob, what the hell, man?"

"I'm sorry, man. I'm sorry."

"It's alright."

"I didn't mean to hurt you, Johnny."

"It's okay."

"You okay, really?"

"You got me good, man."

"Aw, I'm really sorry, man."

He helps me out of the store.

At least we're talking again.

The next day Teresa sends us both back like little boys and makes us pay for all the hot dogs.

20

BIG BEAR REALLY IS A NICE PLACE ONCE YOU GET USED TO IT. Cuckoo clocks are kind of loud but funny. Anger management classes are kind of interesting. My probation officer was a good enough guy, and it's not like I haven't been in treatment before. And if I gotta pee in a cup, I pee in a cup, nothing new about that either.

I landed lucky, landed at Oscar De La Hoya's camp up there in Big Bear. He was generous to let me stay and use his facilities, and his trainer to train me, and get back into shape, getting ready for the fight against Jesse Miranda.

I was in the gym every day, hitting the bags, jumping rope, working with Oscar's trainer on the mitts while Teresa's on the phone trying to convince Paul Chavez to come up to Big Bear.

But Paul says, "no."

He's mad. Teresa tries to convince him.

"Paul. We didn't have a choice to leave. Why don't you come here? Johnny can't be in New Mexico and you know it."

Paul says, "Well, I'm not gonna inconvenience myself just

because Johnny fucked up again. That's his problem."

"What do you want us to do, Paul?"

"That's your problem."

"You're Johnny's manager and trainer."

"Damn right, I am. And you're gonna pay me for being his manager."

"Then we can hire a trainer for Big Bear, Paul, and you can stay manager."

"If you hire a trainer, I will sue you."

"Are you saying, you're not coming to Big Bear to train him, but you still wanna be paid as his trainer?"

"That's exactly what I'm saying."

"No way, Paul. You have a contract. Then you come here and fulfill your contract."

He hung up.

Then he sued us. And then we sued each other. And we sued each other over that for quite a while. But finally the man got paid and had to do nothing in the end.

But I got used to Big Bear. I mean, last time I had spent a lot of time around trees I fell off a mountain. So, here I just stuck to the gym and went to my meetings. My treatment was called "Operation Breakthrough." I had to go to all the meetings you could think of. NA. CA. AA. I can't remember all the letters I went to.

Oscar was around a lot and the two of us spent time together. He's a special, generous guy. A really great human being. He helped me out in so many ways, getting me back on my feet. He even got me endorsements later on.

Oscar's so clean cut and straight forward and so into being healthy. He was always giving me shit for drinking a case of Dr. Pepper every day and eating all those Snickers bars. He believed in doing yoga. He played golf. He took me and Teresa out on the links a couple of times and was real patient with me. He's standing here, explaining over and over again, how to hold the club, how to get the swing right. He kept saying I was too uptight. Said I've got to find a sport that's going to help me relax.

Now, I wasn't going to argue with him, but there are just some things I don't do. And relax is one of them. I feel like I'm on fire most of the time, anyway. Like I got some jet propulsion inside me and the slowest I can go is Mach I. I swear, relaxing literally hurts me.

So, while he's trying to keep me focused on the swing, I'm carjacking the golf cart and doing wheelies in the grass until they kick us off the links. So much for golf.

Big Bear was good to me. It was a time I felt good and healthy and prosperity was beginning to flow for us. And it was so good and abundant that it made me want to share it with the world.

One day Teresa and I were shopping in San Bernardino at the mall, and we're just getting ready to drive back up to Big Bear, when I saw something that tore at my heart so close, that I had to stop the car.

There's this lady and she's real pregnant, and she has a kid in one hand, and a big grocery bag in the other and she's struggling with all of it, walking a long way home.

I make Teresa stop the car and pull over next to her. I wait as she comes up and she's looking at me kind of strange and I come up to her and say, "Here, let me help you with that."

She's trying to hold the groceries back.

"That's okay."

"No, no, no. A woman in your condition, you shouldn't be walking alone like this. You got nobody to help you?"

"Oh, I'm fine."

"You don't got a car?"

"I'm okay walking."

"Let me give you a ride home. My wife and I will give you a ride home."

I take her groceries while she looks confused.

"See, here, that's my wife, Teresa. Teresa, say hello. So what's your name?"

Her name was Rosa.

"Rosa, my wife and I were on our way home and we saw you're walking here all by yourself and we just wanna give you a ride home. Right, Teresa? Teresa, tell her it's okay."

Teresa looks out the window, kind of apologetic.

"It's okay. My husband is always like that. He just wants to help."

She looks between us and then she finally nods.

"Okay. Thank you."

We get in the car. Teresa is driving. I'm leaning back, talking to her, asking her all kinds of questions.

I find out that she's all alone. That her husband disappeared on her a while back. That she doesn't have a car. And that she's trying to support herself and her child, and the new baby on the way.

By the time we get her to her house, she's happy and says thanks and waves, and makes her little daughter wave as we drive off.

But it wouldn't leave me alone. I've got so much and she has nothing. I've been blessed and yet I was there once, holding my mother's hand. My mother who had no one, who was all alone.

And then I start thinking, this could have been my mother. She was all alone, too, raising a child on her own, with no one to help her.

I start saying to Teresa, "She should have a car."

There's a used car lot on the side of the road. I make her pull in.

"Johnny, are you sure about this?"

I said, "Yes. I wanna do this for this woman. I gotta help her out. I have to do it because I can, you know?"

"I know, Johnny."

"You agree?"

"I agree."

So we went in and we bought a little car, a decent car that would run and drive, and we pay for it right there, and I follow Teresa as we drive back to the woman's house and pull up outside.

And she's real surprised to see us again. And then I hand her the keys to the car, and she looks at me, kind of shocked.

"You like it? It's yours."

She starts to cry.

"It's hurts my heart to think of you all alone without a car, having to walk by yourself. Please take this gift."

She couldn't say anything for a long time.

She nods through her tears.

"Thank you. Thank you."

Teresa hugs her. I hug her.

And we drive off as she's waving good-bye.

Now I'm not saying this to make a big thing out of myself. I've given away homes and trailers, probably more than twenty of them in my life to people who needed it at the time. Like to the waitress in Big Bear. She lost her home, her family living in their car. I bought them a thirty thousand dollar trailer and handed them the keys and watched her husband, a six foot four Irish bear of a man, drop to his knees and break down crying. All I asked was that they help someone else out in need. That's how life gets better for us all.

If I could make someone happy with the blessings that I have, I've been more than happy to do it. It's how my mother taught me. It's the generous spirit she had, that I believe in so much.

But Rosa, the lady with no car, was always special to me. It was my way of passing on the love my mother always had for others to someone just like her. By giving the car to this nice lady, I felt I had done something for my mother, too. And that meant more to me than I can tell you right now. It was like she was alive again for one moment.

Like she could still be saved.

21

IN 1995, JACKIE KELLAN WAS THE ONLY KNOWN FEMALE MANAGER AROUND IN THE BOXING WORLD. There was nobody else. But I didn't have a manager or a trainer anymore, and the Jesse Miranda fight needed to be negotiated and promoted and Top Rank wanted a "Manager of Record" in order to let me fight.

This guy, Bob Case, was a good friend of ours, and he comes out to Big Bear, drives up from L.A. to hang with us for a few days and talk about stuff.

Bob and me, we met at Caesars Palace after one of my fights. He was a genuine guy all around. He never wanted a dime from our friendship. He said he wanted to give his advice for free, that it should stay between friends. He wanted his motives to be pure. And he just believed in me and Teresa. He's one of the best men, one of the most beautiful human beings I know. One of the best friends I ever had, and am still fortunate to have.

He was the one who got this idea put out there. He said I should have Teresa start managing me. We needed to set up the next fight. And she should negotiate it with Bob Arum

Mi Vida Loca

who was the head of Top Rank.

"Come on. Why don't you let Teresa handle it? She's handled everything else in your life. She's seen the business now. She's super smart. She's got balls. Let her do it. That way you keep it all in the family. Keep control for yourself. Keep your money. What do you think?"

It was true. Teresa had been there for me all along. She was always looking out for me, giving me advice, saying, "You need this. They're not doing that right." She could always see it and she was always right. So, I knew she already knew my business.

But there wasn't a wife manager anywhere in boxing. It sounded strange. Sounded like you had some kind of a problem. But Bob kept insisting and I knew in my heart he was right. I knew he was right because of who Teresa was. She is a smart, smart woman. And she's handled me. What could be so hard about a couple of promoters?

Bob Arum is known for his smarts. He's Harvard Law educated. He's not your cliché promoter. He's a slick and smart guy who wears glasses and expensive Italian suits.

He was Teresa's first call.

Teresa said, "Bob. This is Teresa. I'm acting as Johnny's manager now. We need to negotiate a new contract because his contract is up."

He says, "You wanna make a deal? Come to Las Vegas and we'll talk about it."

So we drive all the way to Las Vegas, Nevada. Teresa goes inside the office alone and I'm waiting in the waiting room, pacing, messing up their magazines.

She goes inside and sits down and lays a piece of paper across from him and says, "Here's what Johnny wants."

But Bob Arum just blows her off right there. He says, "Listen, you're not telling me what to do. Here's what Johnny's gonna get." And he puts our old contract in front of her.

She said he was so loud and angry, and that she felt so intimidated by him, that she just left that office and came out with the old contract in her hand. I see her close the door. She looks at me and I see her face. She goes out and I follow her outside, because she looks upset.

"What happened in there? Did you get me everything that I asked for?"

She said, "No."

"What did you get me?"

"Same contract."

And she shows me the old contract in her hand.

"What happened?"

"He yelled at me."

I was confused. I followed her down the street and we were quiet for a moment. I had my head down. She looks at me.

"Johnny?"

I can't answer her.

"What's wrong?"

I looked at her.

"Don't you believe in me?"

"Of course I believe in you."

"Well, don't you believe I'm worth more than this?"

"Yeah, I do."

"Well, why don't you do something about it? You're always telling me how they're not treating me right out there. Why don't you do something about it now?"

She didn't answer, but she had a funny face on.

We went to the hotel and stayed the night. But something changed in her. She went back in that office the next day. I had never signed the contract. And she stood up in front of Bob Arum and said, "We're not signing this."

He started yelling at her.

But Teresa said, "First of all, Bob, I'm not your employee. I'm here to offer you talent. You know you have one of the most popular fighters in Johnny."

Bob Arum starts telling her about how we need him, and not the other way around.

So Teresa says, "You know, Bob, if you do not listen to me, then we don't need to talk anymore." And she walked out and shut the door behind her.

I'm waiting outside nervous. I see her face.

"What happened?"

"We got in an argument. We're not signing this deal."

Suddenly I get real nervous.

"What are you doing? You're gonna ruin my career! You got in an argument with Bob Arum?!"

She says, "Johnny, that's what you told me to do! And you were right!"

I say, "No, no, you go in there right now!"

But she refused and wouldn't let me have any contact with Arum or anybody there.

We drive back to Big Bear and two days she gets the call. It's Bob Arum.

"I want to talk to you."

She says, "Well, we came to see you, Bob. Now you come and see us."

And he did. He drove up to Big Bear from Las Vegas. He sat in our living room with the pine trees outside and the cuckoo clock on the wall.

And Teresa was real tough with him.

"Look, this is what we're gonna do. You can take it or leave it."

He was upset, but he took the deal. We got everything we wanted. I was so proud of her. I couldn't believe it.

She was instantly hated in the boxing world. What was the world coming to? Some upstart wife making deals for her husband? I got a lot of hell for it, I can tell you. She got a lot of hell too. But she had doubled my contract. Paul hadn't raised my price for years. So, what can I tell you? She's real smart. But I'm smarter for marrying that woman.

Back in New Mexico, sparks have ignited over my fighting Danny Romero. I was undefeated. Romero won his fights by knock out, known for his punch. Everywhere you looked, there was press about us meeting toe to toe. Everybody wanted to see us in the ring. We even had the same promoters, Top Rank. It was inevitable that we were going to have to show who was the best man.

Danny had been raised in the ghetto like me. Grew up close to where I did, only blocks from my grandparents' house. But he had a mom and a dad and a family to back him, and he was a devout Catholic, and now lived a life of service and good deeds and citizenship. He was handsome and clean cut, and pretty much the opposite of me. He had a father in his life, Danny Romero Sr., who trained him, managed him, and was by his side all the way.

Danny Romero Sr. had actually trained me when I was still young and amateur. Danny Jr. was young then, too young to be boxing, but his dad trained me for quite some time, and we were all friendly.

But all that had changed. When I got suspended from boxing there was no more hope for Albuquerque, there was no more hero, like I had been. And when Danny came along, he filled a void. They needed him and he had come up big. And it bothered me at the time, but now I was back and we were both world champions, and there just wasn't room for the two of us.

The smack-talking started, the trash-talking, the posturing this way and that. Playing it all up in the newspapers and the media. He was disrespecting me. And I started not to like him. His camp was disrespecting me, playing the right and wrong side of the tracks on me. I'm a peaceful guy deep down and I try to love everybody, but don't you ever cross me. He was talking bad about me, about my family, about me being a criminal, about my using drugs, making me out to be nothing more than some kind of gangbanging loser from the hood.

I didn't appreciate it. So I talked back. I told him to meet me in the ring. I told him to meet me in some alley. If he wasn't afraid to show up.

Since we were both with Top Rank, they put us on the same ticket, showing up at the same fights, everyone comparing. Then Danny starts saying the fans showing up are his fans not my fans. I'm saying, "Hey, you're just a kid. I had fans before you were born."

The papers ate all that up and even made a lot more of it than there was. We were on every magazine: "Tapia against Romero." It was unheard of. We were Junior Bantam Weight champions. Only heavyweights make it on the covers of magazines. But something about this fight. The rivalry sold the fight, and people wanted to see a hometown turf war. And that's what it was becoming. It was about who owned Albuquerque. Who would be king.

His people delayed the fight for a long time. Delayed it for three years. They were waiting for me to get old maybe, but three years after I started boxing again, I was stronger and better than ever. So they were delaying, and the press was getting hotter and hotter, and every week you read something about it in the Albuquerque Journal. But no matter how hard we pressed them to step up and fight, no matter how close we got, there would be something to slow it down again, something to keep it from happening.

Romero had lost against Willy Salazar in 1995 just months before I knocked Willy Salazar out cold in nine rounds. I dedicated the fight to Danny Romero, just to make a point. But still it took years for us to meet in the ring.

The Romeros went to Top Rank and tried to make them chose between me and them. They said they would walk if they didn't drop me. Top Rank chose me and told them to walk. So bad feelings got worse.

It took another year to get that fight on the canvas. I wanted it to be in Albuquerque, Danny refused.

He said he was gonna knock me out in the fourth round into the fourth row, and then my fans were gonna kill him, because it was gonna be that devastating. I was saying, "Bring it on, wherever you wanna do it." I wanted him so bad by this time.

April 30th, 1997, we announced the fight in Las Vegas at the Hilton Hotel. I walk in and Danny's there, and I'm so pumped up. He gives me a look and I couldn't stop myself, all that stuff he'd been saying came back to me, and I jumped him. Cops had to separate us. Papers wrote, "Tapia attacks Romero." It was a big circus. From that moment on, they kept us completely separate. Separate weigh-ins. Separate press conferences.

Now all there was left was to train for the fight. And you couldn't have had two more different approaches there, either. I was in my usual chaotic state. I changed trainers three times. Emanuel Stewart, Jesse Reid, and finally stuck with Eddie Futch, a legendary trainer, and a great guy.

Most of the time I didn't even run to train for a fight. For this one I did run. But I didn't change anything else in my habits. While Danny had a nutritionist, and special sports doctors and a special diet, I was eating out every day, eating french fries, Snickers bars, drinking my Dr Pepper.

Teresa's saying, "My God, Johnny. Don't you think we should change something?"

"Why?" I said. "This is what I've always done."

Teresa was getting nervous, too, because I had always told her that I wasn't ever gonna lose to Danny Romero, that I would kill myself if I lost to Danny Romero.

I told Danny, too. "You're gonna have to kill me. 'Cause I'm willing to die for this fight. Are you?" It was my pride. It was Albuquerque. A pride thing for me. I was fighting for my fans. I wasn't gonna let them down.

The fight was scheduled at the Hilton in Las Vegas. They pulled out last minute. Said they were afraid of my fans. This was just after the Tyson and Holyfield fight, where Tyson had bit Holyfield's ear. People were all skittish in boxing. They knew I was in league with Tyson. They knew we were friendly at least. They didn't know we were roommates once upon a time. It did me make think about how amazing it was. Here we were, me and Tyson, years later, dominating the Las Vegas boxing scene. And now the Hilton just assumed that me and Danny Romero, or maybe just my fans, were gonna launch a full scale gang war.

So Top Rank put the fight together at the "Thomas and Mack Center." They only sold eight thousand seven hundred tickets. In Albuquerque it would have sold out. They put SWAT teams up in the arena. They had double security.

Mi Vida Loca

Twenty or thirty cops in riot gear. They had metal detectors at the door. There was talk of a bomb threat. It was a crazy scene.

My dressing room was mobbed. With Paul Chavez out of the picture, he couldn't keep everybody out anymore. So it was crazy in there, and that's just how I liked it. People coming in and out, wishing me good things, saying hello, saying they're praying for me. I'm cranking the music loud, dancing in the room. Beto Martinez is my cut man and he keeps making me sit down long enough to wrap my hands.

Most boxers have it real quiet in their rooms before a fight. It's like a library in there, everybody concentrating hard, serious. You can bet the nutritionist and sports masseuse and sports therapist were all talking to Danny with quiet respectful voices. But, me, I had a party going on. I like to make a lot of noise before a fight, and on that night I was really pumped up. I got the Mexican music playing loud. Ranchera music. Al Hurricane. Music that's all about fighting and rebels and honor and craziness.

My grandpa had come from Albuquerque. He was rooting for me again. He was the only one. He came into the dressing room to wish me luck. He's the one who told me the rest of my family was there, too, but they were all wearing Danny Romero t-shirts, if you can believe it. It's sure been a love-hate thing with them for me. So, at that time they were still mad at me for some reason or other. It was always about what I had said, or supposedly said to the press about my family. But that night I got to hug my grandpa and told him I was

208

gonna dedicate the fight to my mom.

I'm dancing all around the room, yelling hello to whoever comes inside, shadow boxing, loosening up, hugging more people coming in. I'm just making a lotta noise, and the party juices me up. Then it comes time for me to change into my shorts, and all the ladies have to leave the room. I get into my outfit and I have a priest there and he says a blessing for the fight. I kneel down, people beside me, all of us blessed for the fight. And then it was show time.

When Danny came into the arena the whole place went up in booing. They booed him so loud it was deafening. Nobody expected it to be quite like that. A lot of people had thought Danny had taken Albuquerque from me. I had made so much trouble, been in and out of jail, in and out of rehab. Who could blame anybody for thinking that? But the crowd that night gave me an overwhelming vote.

I came out to my new songs, a ranchera called, "Entierrame Cantando," that goes, "Solo, solo, I am all alone in the world, There's only me, I know I'm gonna die today, I don't fear dying, And whenever God is ready for me, Then I'll go and I'll go singing, And for those I leave behind, I don't want any crying, I don't want any mourning, Just bury me singing…"

My second song was the one I played for my mother. My good friend, Darren Cordova, a beautiful singer who I am honored to know a long time, he wrote a song for my mother called, "Te Estraño, Mama," which means "I love you, I miss you, Mama." I still play those two songs today.

The minute I show myself, the whole place cheered so loud, I couldn't hear myself think. It was just crazy. Amazing.

It took a long time to make it to the ring. There were so many people, everyone reaching out, trying to shake my hand, a crowd pushing up as I am walking to the ring.

Danny is there, waiting for me, tense. I get in the ring with him and we stare each other down. The whole arena, whistling, yelling, booing, and chanting "Johnny, Johnny, Johnny."

Everyone had predicted the fight for Romero. Eight out of ten people picked Danny to be the winner. But from the first round on, I showed that I was not gonna be outdone. I schooled Danny on what it was to be a real fighter. I think Danny never expected me to be that fast. He had to look for me half the time. I knew he had a powerful punch, and I knew I was gonna have to show up and fight him for real. But my speed was so quick, so blinding, that he just couldn't keep up with me. For the full twelve rounds he was literally trying to find me. And I was driven to win. All that stuff before the fight, I was really charged up, I wasn't gonna lose. By everybody's guess, Danny was supposed to knock me out. But when he got in the ring he just couldn't do anything with me. He was frustrated, his corner was frustrated, they were taunting me during the fight. But I knew I had it early on, I had the feeling, and I knew I had the fans behind me. And the fans gave me strength.

A twelve round decision. Unanimous. I won the fight. The crowd went crazy. Crazy. The chanting so loud, "Johnny,

Johnny, Johnny, Johnny!" I tried to go to Danny, to give him a hug. He and his father turned their backs on me. I had to let it go.

There were no gang fights that night. There was no violence. In fact, Albuquerque streets were empty that night. They probably recorded their lowest crime rate ever.

I was crowned King of the Junior Bantam Weights. I was a two time world champion. I hugged my grandpa when he came into the ring after my winning. I handed him the belt, "This is for you, Grandpa." Dedicated that fight to his daughter, my mom.

I hugged my wife. She's the one who had gotten me here. I had sure made it hard for her at times, but she had fought for me, and she managed me to this place, and in that moment it all seemed worth it. I told her how much I loved her. We did it. Together. And it changed our lives. Forever.

22

La abundancia mata la gana.
Abundance kills desire.

THE ONLY THING THAT EVER REALLY BOTHERED ME ABOUT BEING POOR AS A KID WAS HAVING TO WEAR BAD SHOES. Hand me down shoes. Shoes from "Ray's Five and Ten" discount store, plastic ones, imitation sneakers, not the nice, fancy Converse other kids were wearing. I hated not having new shoes. I hated having shoes with holes. It would get so bad, me and Raymond would go down to the roller skating rink and wait 'til everybody was out skating and we'd each steal any pair of shoes that fit us, and leave our old ones behind. I didn't think about whether that was right or wrong then. Having broken, worn out shoes was wrong. And it wasn't fair. Why could they have them and not us? All those people who could afford to go roller skating probably could afford a new pair of shoes. In the ghetto it's all about survival, what you have and what you don't have. Whatever it is, you know you don't have it, and other people do. People up on the hills. People on the other side of the Rio

Grande. For me being rich meant having nice shoes.

Once I was making money in the hundreds of thousands, I could buy all the shoes I wanted. Money still didn't make sense. It was like play money. It wasn't real.

Teresa made sure we saved, Teresa made sure it wasn't all lost the minute it came in. She had us buy houses, improve our living situation, make investments.

But money is not my god.

I was happy as long as I could go to buy a closet full of sneakers, and go back the next week and buy some more. For me, that meant I had made it.

The Romero fight changed our lives. It brought real abundance. It put me on every magazine cover you can imagine. Put everybody on notice. Suddenly I was in the league of the heavyweights.

I had so much press, so many interviews, so much attention, and still when our contract with Top Rank was over and we went to negotiate a new one, Top Rank didn't want to increase the pay. So Teresa got into it with Bob Arum, again.

Bob tells her that she should be grateful for what we're getting, and that he'll be real nice and throw in something extra, and he hands me some keys and tells me to look outside, where there's a brand new Lexus in the parking lot.

"That's your car. Just sign the contract."

I handed him back the keys. Just 'cause I ate bread and mustard for breakfast, didn't make me a fool.

They say, "Boxing is the red light district of sports." Promoters sometimes take advantage of the poverty many boxers come from. And why not? It's life in the big city and it's part of boxing, it's part of the game. I hold no grudges. Bob Arum is a successful man, and we've been in business many times since that time.

But when Bob Arum tries to bait me with a Lexus, my wife gets real mad.

"You think we're some kind of street people, Bob? You think we're gonna jump to a car? We can afford to buy our own car. How dare you insult us like that? And if you can afford to buy us a car, then that means that I screwed up somewhere. Because there shouldn't be any money for that car there. I missed it somewhere and that pisses me off."

They really got into it. Again. It's those times, I get to let somebody else fight my fight for me. When my wife gets tough with these promoters, I stay out of it because I know she can handle it better than I could ever handle it. I'd just start punching somebody and then we'd all be in trouble. She can fight with words.

"You need me," he tells us.

"No, Bob, you didn't get in that ring. Johnny did. Did I see you get your ass off that chair? No. All you do is sit there."

"If it wasn't for me--"

"If it wasn't for Johnny, there would be no winning. You can put him in that ring, but it takes him to win the fights."

She had a point. I was ten years undefeated by then.

So we walked away. Bob was still mad, telling us we're making the most money with him we'll ever make, and that if I leave, I would never fight again.

Mi Vida Loca

Well, it took one phone call to Don King to change that tune. He told us to come meet him in New York. Don was on trial for something or other, and he was real busy, but he was gonna make time for us. So Teresa, Robert, and me, head out to the Big Apple.

She went into Don King's office. And, you know, Don King is larger than life. My wife is a petite, feminine, beautiful lady. She walks into this room and sits across from Don sitting on his throne, and three other guys in the room. He's got Bobby Goodman, his matchmaker, Carl King, his son, and Charles Lomax, one of his attorneys.

But Teresa had faced down Bob Arum and survived it. And she'd handled me, too. That beautiful girl was only twenty four years old and had already lived a few life times. She had been schooled tough by now. And there was no way that a Don King was going to intimidate her.

Don King is reclining in his chair, and he's acting all relaxed and he says to her, "Here's what we're gonna do."

He slides a contract over to her.

"Sign this here contract and we can start it today."

She looked at it and said, "There's no numbers in this contract."

"We can fill them out later."

"No, we're gonna do that right now."

"Oh, sweetheart. You gotta understand that you just need to get this thing signed. I got lots of stuff for Johnny to do. I'm gonna make him bigger than he is now. And that Arum…"

The Crazy Life of Johnny Tapia

He hates Bob Arum with a passion.

"No, Don. Here are our numbers. If you do these numbers, then we'll sign."

He looked insulted and said, "I can't do that."

So she said, "This is pointless. Let's stop right here." And she gets up and starts to walk away. But Don King says, "Hold on, little girl. Sit back down."

She faces him, "Listen, Don, I'm not here to waste your time. But I don't wanna waste mine either. If I didn't think this was doable, I wouldn't be asking."

He looks at her.

"So how much signing bonus do you want?"

"Three hundred thousand."

There's a long silence. He shakes his head and laughs.

Finally he says, "Okay. You got a deal."

They shook hands on it. She smiles at him.

"Well, Don, as I look at it, all promoters are crooks. If you're gonna get screwed, you might as well get screwed by somebody you like."

The room gets real quiet. Everybody looking at Don for a reaction. Then he starts to laugh real hard, and he's got this big laugh, and then everybody else laughs, too. And he says, "I like this little girl."

After that he was great. Took Teresa under his wing and really taught her the ropes. Got me much further than I'd ever been before. He just catapulted me into a whole new arena. Put my name out there with all the other big fighters. He'd be talking about Holyfield or Tyson to the press and say,

"But Johnny Tapia. That Johnny Tapia. That's a name you gotta remember." He got me an exclusive deal with Showtime.

He was good to us. As bad a reputation as people want to give him, you always see him stay in touch with people, try and help fighters out, get them jobs after they retire. He was a friend. And he really made it happen for us then.

And everything changed from there. Suddenly I've got a closet full of shoes. Probably fifty pairs or more. Nikes, Pumas, Adidas. We traded in our matching blue Camaros we had at the time and I bought a brand new Yukon SUV, and I got Teresa a red convertible Corvette. We buy a big house in Las Vegas, Nevada. Four bedrooms, four bathrooms. Nice house in the Driftwood Estates. We called it the "Driftwood house." It was thirty five hundred square feet and it had a pool.

We'd wake up in that house and Teresa would say, "I don't feel like doing laundry today."

So I'd take her to the mall and we'd just buy more clothes instead of washing.

We went jewelry shopping and I'd get us his-and-hers twenty five thousand dollar Rolex watches.

We'd get bored and just get on a plane and go to London, Paris, Scotland, New York, California, Texas, and home to New Mexico.

I wore Armani suits. She wore Armani dresses. I bought her Gucci purses and Gucci shoes. I built a bigger and better shoe closet.

I had four fights with Don King and I won them, defending my title. I defeated Andy Agosto in Pompano Beach,

Florida. I beat Rodolfo Blanco in Albuquerque. Don had the idea to have the fight on my birthday and we set a record for ticket sales at The Pit, broke state records for attendance and live gate, over ten thousand seats. Don wanted to make a real big show of it and he had me jump through a false wall for my entrance. The place want insane for it. I fought and won and celebrated my birthday, I was thirty one.

The papers wrote, "Tapia Throws Birthday Bash To Record Crowds." Carl King was quoted saying, "You rarely find this kind of support for a fighter in the United States. Maybe in Europe or South America, but not here." Everybody was asking me about how I liked selling so many tickets, and how I liked making so much money.

It made me uncomfortable to be honest. I said, "I'm just honored to have the love of the fans." I loved to feel the warmth of the embrace of my hometown city, when three years before they were ready to disown me over Danny Romero. It was overwhelming.

But I could also feel the presence of my family that time. And it was different now. I came back a star. A big star. And my family was living in the ghetto. My brother Raymond was in prison for murder. My grandma wasn't talking to me, wouldn't let me call. My grandpa didn't come to the fight. My family wasn't talking to me, again, or still.

I heard from Randall that my grandpa was still running every day, working out all the time. And that ever since he had quit drinking, he had become quieter, and now my Grandma Ester was the "Master of the Dirt," and she held firm control.

I missed my grandpa, but my grandma didn't want me coming over. Her, Helen, all of them. They had even turned my grandpa against me. If I called, she said I was dead to the family. Many bad feelings had built up.

After my sudden success, and the money coming in, things got harder between us. I sent them checks all the time. I paid to fix up their house. I paid off their cars. We spent Christmas wrapping a hundred presents for all the kids and grandkids and great grandkids, and they sent them back.

I had given an interview a while back with Jim Rome. It brought up a lot of memories about my mother. I talked about my childhood and how we were poor, and how my aunts were in jail for heroin. Well, that didn't go over well with my family. The media put a lot of pressure on them. Suddenly I was talking about them, and it didn't always make them look good, and they hated being talked about. Suddenly they were under a microscope. Every time I have an interview and somebody asked me about my family, somebody would call them afterwards and ask them what they thought about what I said. Where I had the benefits of fame and the drawbacks, too, they had only the drawbacks that come with fame, just by being associated with me.

My grandmother was furious.

"How could you say we were poor?"

"Grandma, we were poor."

"You always had food on the table, didn't you? We took

you in. We raised you, we fed you, we clothed you. And now you're talking about your aunts being drug addicts and being in jail. Talking about your family to the whole world. Making us look bad. You said you had nothing when you married Teresa. And that's not true. You always had us."

"I was sleeping in parks. You kicked me out of the house, remember?"

"You're ungrateful, you always were. Broke your grandfather's heart. Now you gotta shame us in public."

"I love grandpa. I will always love him. He trained me. He taught me. He started me. I never forget that, Grandma. I always tell him I love him and I love you. I love my family."

"You abandoned your family. You abandoned all of us."

"You don't let me come and visit you. You hang up on me when I call."

"That's right and don't call anymore. We don't wanna talk to you no more. You're not a Tapia no more. We don't want nothing to do with you."

"Grandma, come on, I love you—"

But she hung on me. She wanted nothing to do with me. It was one of many times that I was shut out from the family.

At home, the fame and the money were starting to cause problems, too. All the money made the partying so much more accessible and fun. And I was still partying and with a lot of cash in your pocket, you can really make some trouble. Now I was hanging out in casinos and riding around in limos, eating in expensive restaurants. I wasn't

Mi Vida Loca

hiding in the mechanic's pit of some chop shop. It was a lot more civilized, and I could lie to myself easier, and justify it better.

So between our shopping sprees, I would disappear again. Then I'd come back and take Teresa shopping again. I would come back and buy her five hundred dollar shoes. I told her to have her own suits designed and made for her. I bought her diamond rings and Cartier watches. I was bribing her with material things just to buy my freedom.

And she knew it.

Pretty soon she started saying how she didn't want those things. How she was happy when we were living back in a four-room house in Albuquerque.

"At least you were clean then. That's all I ever wanted."

"Why are you always complaining?"

"I don't want to trade my happiness for material things."

"You have a beautiful home. You have beautiful cars, money, jewelry. What more do you want from me?"

"I want you."

She'd look at me.

"I can't curl up with a hundred dollar bill."

I didn't know what to say to her.

"I need my freedom, Teresa. You have to let me have my freedom."

I never saw how drugs had taken all my freedom away. The drugs were the only thing making me unfree. But my demons were always only a short step behind me, just on my heels. And they had caught up with me once again.

So Teresa stayed home, ran the business, kept a good face on things, managed it all, while I went out and partied.

I never meant to hurt her. I wouldn't be alive without her. She's never deserved all the trouble I've been. But something had such a hold on me, and it just wouldn't let go.

23

MY MOTHER WAS MURDERED WHEN SHE WAS THIRTY-TWO. I didn't think I would outlive her. I never thought I'd make it past my own thirty second birthday. I didn't even want to make it past her thirty-second birthday.

After turning thirty-one, I could feel that time was coming on. It started growing in the back of my mind, and it was always there in my head. I was counting down the days, weeks, and months to the time that I would be the age she was when she died. I started to feel that time was running out for me.

The interview with Jim Rome had brought up a lot of memories, too. He was asking about my mother and her death and my childhood, asking about who killed my mother. Didn't I know? Didn't they ever find out who did it? Why didn't anybody know who killed her? Why didn't they ever find him?

It bothered me that I couldn't answer these questions. I had always just thought there was no way to know. They must have tried to find him. They just couldn't.

And then I was also busy struggling to survive for so long,

and fighting for my career, fighting for my life, fighting for my marriage.

But success had come and opened up some thinking time, some time to feel more things from the past, less distracted by survival. I had already achieved my dream. Everything ahead was just going to be more and better of the same thing, but I had already made it to where I wanted to be.

So there was room for the old feelings to come up stronger again. Feelings that had never gone away.

"Teresa. I want to know what happened to my mom."

Teresa looks at me, kind of nervous. I've talked to her about finding the man who killed my mother before. I always said that when I found him, I was going to say good-bye to my family, kiss my wife farewell, and I was going to go and kill him. But that was the anger. The anger that was alive in me all the time. My desire for revenge. But now I wanted justice for my mom. Now, I could feel that I needed to put it to rest.

"Johnny, that's all over now," she said.

"But I need to know."

"What will it change? It won't bring her back."

"I need to know who killed her, Teresa. Will you help me?"

"Johnny, I'm scared of what it'll do to you."

"I need closure. Will you help me get closure?"

She looks at me, and finally nods, "Yes. I will."

We didn't talk about it after that. She did everything on her own. Contacted the District Attorney in Albuquerque.

Wrote letters to the police department. Called our attorney, Michael Mozes, to have him dig things up. Even got it on "Unsolved Mysteries." But nobody could find much. There would be hints of things, looking back through the file. She puzzled out the case for a while. There were tips that led nowhere.

She talked to Detective Bobby H. Rohlfs Jr. He was the son of the detective who was on the case years ago. He said he would try and help. He said that case always bothered his father, but his father had died. People were nice. People wanted to help. But there was nothing. No news for a long time. Maybe it was too long ago. There are some things you can't get back no matter how hard you try. So, for a while I forgot about it all.

I had to get ready for my third title fight. The WBA belt. King put it together with Nana Konadu from Ghana. I was going to go up in weight, couldn't stay at 115, junior bantamweight, anymore. Had to go to 118, to bantamweight, and that meant facing a harder fighter like Konadu.

He was a heavy hitter and I knew I had to outbox him. Freddie Roach was training me at the new training camp we had built in Ruidoso and he had me train special just for this fight. He said, "Konadu's an exceptional fighter. He's got a lot of power and he's unusual because he never stops coming forward. You're gonna outbox him, Johnny. You're gonna take away that power."

So we trained at lateral movement. He had me going side to side all the time. Romero was a fighter like that, too.

Relying on power. But I was able to hold Romero off. But Konadu was somebody who just wouldn't stop coming, and I was gonna have to keep him off balance. I was gonna have to flurry and move left and right. We trained hard for that.

The fight was in Atlantic City at the Convention Center. It was on Showtime. A big deal, fighting in Atlantic City. Never been there before. Big press. Big show. A nice purse.

It ended up being a fight of skill, more than flash. I worked it all twelve rounds and won the unanimous decision. But it was not a crowd pleaser. Konadu was patient and I kept to my strategy. The crowd booed. Didn't like that it wasn't more guts and gore. But in the end I was happy. Boring or not, I was bringing home the WBA title.

The night after the fight we're still in Atlantic City. Posters for the fight were still plastered all over town, you couldn't look anywhere and not see my face. I had to stop lots of times, shake hands, sign autographs.

I was happy. Happy with the fight. Happy to be surrounded by family and friends. Happy to greet the fans and do a little shopping.

Teresa was with me, and Robert G, who's my permanent corner man. We had our good friends Al and Cathy Ortiz with us, too. They're some special people, who had come into our lives. Spiritual people who have supported us all the way, advised us, put their own lives aside just to help. Teresa's sister, Eva, and her husband, Chris, were there too.

When I'm out in public I usually have a big group with me. I like to bring people along, make it an experience for them. But also, I feel best when I have people surrounding me, good friends close to me. Al and Rob were also there just for some protection. We take care of each other. But whether they're protecting me from somebody else, or protecting me from myself, you never know.

We're walking the boardwalk because the girls wanted to shop for trinkets and memorabilia, when I see a commotion under a bridge close by. There was some homeless man, must have been in his seventies, being beat up by twelve gang kids, pounding in on this man. He's doubled over, they're beating him with fists and sticks. At that moment it didn't matter that my face was on posters all over Atlantic City, how big a purse I had made, what kind of a star I was. It didn't matter that Don King was my promoter, or how high I had risen in the boxing world. If I see somebody in trouble, I see someone being mistreated, I have to step in.

I run over there.

Teresa is yelling, "No, Johnny, no!"

But I was already off, charging the gang, waving my arms, "What the hell are you doing?! Leave that guy alone!"

These were big gang dudes, and they hardly noticed me, bantamweight, small as I am. But they sure noticed me when I reached them and started taking them out, one by one.

Rob and Al have joined me now, and they're helping, too. Pretty soon there's sirens. Teresa is standing there, "Johnny, come on. The cops are coming!"

I didn't even hear her. Too busy taking out these thugs.

Next thing I know, cops are grabbing me and Robert, the

homeless man, and the gang guys, the ones who aren't out cold on the ground. Everybody yelling, shouting. The cops say, "What's going on here?"

The cops hold on to me across from one of the gang bangers. The kid looks in my face and says, "You think you're so tough? Let's see you hit me now!"

So I did. He asked.

It didn't matter that some police officer had his hands on me. I punched the guy.

Teresa's yelling, "Johnny, no!"

The gangbanger is shouting at the cops, "Assault and battery! Arrest him! Arrest this guy!"

Meanwhile the homeless man has his voice back and he's yelling, too.

"You can't arrest him. He saved my life. This is the best man I ever met. He saved my life. This is a hero. You can't arrest him."

Now I don't have the best track record with the cops. But that's something that fame and success has actually changed. I was all ready to be arrested. But this officer looks at me and shakes my hand.

"You're a hell of a fighter, Mr. Tapia. It's an honor to meet you. You fought a hell of a fight last night. But not everybody's gonna understand what happened here. You gotta give me your word that you're gonna disappear right now. Just get outta here, okay? And stay outta trouble while you're in Atlantic City, you hear me?"

My new best friend. Things sure had changed.

"Sure, officer. Thank you very much. You're a good human being."

I hugged the homeless man, then hugged the policeman, and went on my way. So much for Atlantic City. I did my good deed. But I haven't been back.

Two months later I turned thirty two.

24

I WASN'T SUPPOSED TO GET THE CALL. Teresa had told Detective Rohlfs, "Do not talk to Johnny yourself." He was supposed to tell only her, and she made that very clear. If they ever found the murderer she wanted to be the one to tell me.

It was early 1998. Don King was back on trial again and he couldn't focus on his fighters. He had taken me a long way, given me a lot, got me another world title, raised my purse, got me all this exposure, got me on Showtime, made me a world class fighter. He was great. But his troubles were taking him over. My contract was up. So it was time to move on.

We went back to Bob Arum, who gave me a two-fight deal. Showtime. I fought in Albuquerque. Alberto Martinez. Knocked him out in the first round.

The second fight was going to be with a young guy named Paulie Ayala. He'd never won a title before. He was known to be a smart and tough fighter, but I knew I could outbox him.

He was a nice kid. We went on a press junket together and

his own little boy said I was his favorite fighter. He was so cute. Made me want to have kids again.

Teresa and I always talked about having kids, wished for it, hoped for it, but it seemed like things were always too crazy to think about that. We had taken in her sister's son for a while, Jonathan. They were going through hard times. Jonathan was like my son, but he went back to his family one day. And I missed him. And I still wanted kids.

That's how life was. It was kind of normal. I had my career. My wife. Our houses. Our lives together. A fight coming up.

I was training in Ruidoso, training with Freddie Roach. It was two weeks away from the fight, scheduled for Las Vegas. It was my first time headlining Showtime, pay-per-view. A big deal. I was defending the WBA title that I had just won six months before from Nana Konadu.

But two weeks out from the Ayala fight, nobody was expecting this call.

I was in the gym, working out with Robert on the mitts, when the phone rings. The phone was connected to Teresa's office and to the gym, too. It was ringing and ringing.

Teresa was on another call and she wasn't picking up. I never pick up the phone. But it wouldn't stop ringing. And there was just a flash feeling I had. Usually I would have let it stop ringing. But this time, I picked it up.

"Who's this!"

There was a silence on the other end.

A man's voice. "Hello?"

"Yeah, who's this?"

"My name is Detective Rohlfs, Albuquerque Police."

I can tell you, I had a pit in my stomach right away. First of all, any call from the police is not a call I ordinarily like to take. But this one sounded different. My mind starts reeling.

"I'm trying to reach Teresa Tapia."

"She's not here right now."

"Then I'll call back."

"You can talk to me. This is Johnny Tapia."

"I need to talk to her directly, Mr. Tapia."

My mind is racing, my heart is pounding in my chest.

"This is about my mother, isn't it?"

He didn't answer right away.

"You found the murderer, didn't you?"

"So then you know about it?"

"I know all about it. You can tell me."

There is another silence.

"I don't know. She was real specific."

"No, man. We talked about everything. If there's something you have to say, you can say it to me. You're talking about my own mother, you know?"

He's very polite, "Of course. I understand, sir. You're right about that. And, yes, you're right. We did find out who killed your mother."

My guts are wrenched. I'm feeling tight. I'm barely breathing.

I turn around and look at Robert. He hasn't noticed anything. He's packing the bags up, folding my towels, his back to me.

"Tell me. Tell me who it is."

Robert is walking from the gym. I'm all alone in that moment.

"We have an individual's name. Some credible information came together and we believe, with certainty, that the man who killed your mother was a man named Richard Espinoza."

Time seems frozen.

"Do you know where he is?"

"He is deceased."

"Deceased?"

"He was killed in a car accident six months ago."

My hands are clammy. I feel all the strength leave my body. I feel like the world is folding up underneath me. My knees feel rubbery. My hand is clenched on the phone receiver.

"So he's dead now?"

"Yes, he is."

"And you're sure about it?"

"Yes, we are, sir."

I don't have anything else to say.

"Would you tell your wife to call me please? I should talk to her as well."

I don't remember if I answered. I don't know what happened in that moment. I put the phone down.

There's no word to describe how I felt except blackness. Everything went black. Black in my mind. Black in my soul. All those years, all that rage coming up inside me. All those memories, all that focus on what I would do someday when I found the killer. It was all gone. And my mother was dead. In that moment, she was really dead.

I walked straight up to my room, shut the door, and wouldn't let anybody inside.

Pretty soon I hear Teresa at the door. She's knocking, then pounding on it.

"Johnny, what's going on? Johnny, let me in! Johnny, open up the door! Johnny, talk to me!"

I can't talk. I can't move. If I had had a gun right then, I would have blown my brains away.

I stopped training. I stopped all preparations for the fight. I cancelled everything. I stayed in my room. Didn't want to talk to anyone.

Teresa is trying to talk to me.

"Johnny, you need to train. You need to make weight."

I still had to get my weight down.

"I'll eat ice chips. I'll make weight."

"Johnny, you need to eat. You need to train."

"Just put me in a phone booth with Ayala. I'll be there. I'll be there to fight. I'll show up and I'll give them everything they want. But I don't wanna see anybody until then. Send everybody home. I wanna be alone."

And I stayed that way. Two weeks. A huge depression over me. I couldn't be close to the people I loved. I was filled with too much hatred and blackness and confusion. I didn't want to be alive. Nothing mattered anymore. My mother was dead. And there was nothing I could do about it anymore.

All those years, my mother's death was a daily thought in

Mi Vida Loca

my mind. All those years I had held those feelings inside. Years of waking up at night with nightmares. Years of wondering who the killer was. Years of hoping for justice one day, hoping to get revenge for what was taken from me. And now that was taken, too.

Ten years after brutally murdering my mother, Richard Espinoza walked out of a bar at midnight, totally drunk, and walked into the street and right into a car. He was hit, thrown into the air and run over by another car and another after that. It took three cars to take that evil from this world.

I had wanted that man so bad. But now he was dead. It was all over.

The day of the fight came. I had been in my room for two weeks, with the blinds drawn, alone.

And now I wanted to hurt somebody. Now it was gonna be Paulie Ayala since he was brave enough to face me in the ring.

It was a hard night. A lot of things were going wrong. Teresa shielded me from a lot of trouble, like she always does, so I can just concentrate on the fight. But this time some guy from Top Rank was in the back, talking in on me, coming up with a bunch of police, warning me that they were not gonna put up with any gangster tactics. I didn't know what the hell they were talking about. But they made a lot of tension happen. They were putting a heavy muscle on for no reason. This wasn't the Romero fight. Maybe it was the Bones Adams contract that I didn't want to sign. Maybe it was that I was no longer under contract with Top Rank after this fight, and

Paulie Ayala was. I understand it. You have two horses in the running, and one of them is no longer yours. Which one are you gonna support? But I don't know what made the air so thick with tension. It seems like people were trying to stir up trouble on all fronts.

I was so aggravated with this guy from Top Rank, who is no longer living, by the way. Which, by the way, I had nothing to do with.

But I was so aggravated that I went into that ring very angry, angrier than I've ever been in any fight. I've always used my anger to give me strength, but now I was like a warrior that had gone into seclusion to meditate on the final battle. And that final battle was here. I entered the ring. I shoved Paulie Ayala just to put him on notice.

He would later say he had never seen so much hatred in anyone's eyes, like he saw in mine that night.

I was there to fight. I was there to get the job done.

My grandpa was there. Actually came to see me fight in Las Vegas again. Teresa had been talking to the family about my mother's murder. It brought my grandpa back to me for a little while. And here he was, standing in my corner. Eighty three years old. After the gangster warning, and me shoving Paulie, security came up and hauled him away, handled this eighty three year old man so roughly, he was covered in bruises, his whole body, afterwards.

They also arrested Rob right out of my corner. When I shoved Paulie and the two sides start going at it, he was waving his towel to get the crowd cheering. Got him put in handcuffs and taken hauled away.

It was a crazy night.

Still I fought my twelve rounds and I was all business. I was all fight. I stayed in there and used the little poem I had learned and always used. "Lead with the speed, follow with the power." We stood toe to toe all night. You could have put this fight in a phone booth.

I didn't give them my usual antics and joking. I wasn't as funny as I usually was. I didn't kiss anybody on the head. It was me without the clowning around. All slugging.

We went all twelve rounds. Everyone I know had me the winner. We stood as the crowd cheered and whistled, restless, waiting for the judges decision.

It took a long time.

Bobby Czyz, Steve Albert and Ferdie Pacheco ran out of things to say before the judges came back.

Jimmy Lennon takes the microphone.

We're all standing in the ring, our hands held up, both of us, assuming the win.

Jimmy Lennon reads the numbers.

A unanimous decision. The judges had it 116-112, 115-113, 115-113. For Ayala.

I was stunned.

I looked at Teresa and she just shook her head.

I couldn't believe it.

I hadn't lost that fight. I knew I hadn't lost that fight.

There were boos raining down on Ayala. The crowd let Ayala know they were on my side from the beginning. But when the decision went to him, the place went up in arms, an angry crowd. Stunned crowd.

And I knew it was a close fight, but I honestly thought I won.

Ayala would later say that it was the fight of his life. He would say that I landed forty punch combinations, like he had never seen anybody punch as fast and as vicious as I did. I knew I had come to fight, and that's exactly what I gave him.

The fight was later voted "Fight of the Year." Ayala put up a good fight himself. Paulie was tough and I gave him all the respect.

Bob Arum and I parted ways at that time. My contract had expired. I went on to others. Back to Don King for a while, too.

But Bob and me, we ultimately came back together. They were there from the beginning. No matter the ups and downs, they brought me up from the beginning.

We've worked together since then. Many times. What can I say? If you let the business eat you up, it will. In the end it's just business, nothing personal. You take it as it comes to you and you move on.

It was the first loss of my career. I had always been compared to Rocky Marciano. People were always saying, I was gonna stay undefeated. I was undefeated for eleven straight years. It seemed like it was gonna last forever. I never considered losing. Never considered that I would lose at all. My first loss stunned everybody. Including me.

But I had other things to go home and think about.

25

THIS IS HOW MY MOTHER DIED. On the night she went dancing, my mother took a friend with her who everybody called Lola. Her name was Dolores Castillo and sometimes people called her "Bulldozer," because of how she looked. Scary. Lola was a heroin addict, a short, dumpy girl who didn't really have a lot going on. Virginia was protective of her though, and she was being generous to her. She wanted to help Lola out. My mother didn't want to go that night, but she wanted to keep her promise. Lola didn't have a car of her own, and my mom was Lola's ride.

They went to the "Cow Palace" on Central Avenue. There they met my mother's boyfriend at the time, Richard Espinoza. He was still wearing his blue custodian's uniform from his work at a high school. It was Friday night. He had just been paid for two weeks work, and his pay, one hundred and eighty dollars, was still in his wallet. He was ready to party that night and he was already drinking heavily before they met him.

For a while Richard was still only half drunk and he and my mother and Lola and some other guy were sitting drinking beers. Everyone except my mother. Richard was drinking his favorite Schlitz Malt Liquor and smoking Winston cigarettes.

Later, when Richard was too drunk to talk, my mother was dancing by herself on the dance floor, and Richard was alone, drinking at the bar. Richard was talking to the bartender who was concerned about how drunk he was. The bartender was refusing to serve him, and Richard became angry. Lola was standing by Richard when he lost his footing, fell to the floor, passed out.

Lola called Virginia over.

"Virginia, come get your man."

The two of them lifted Richard up with the help of the security guard named Richard McCain. McCain said they'd better get him home. He helped them get Richard out to his car which was parked out in front on the street.

Virginia told Lola to follow her in Helen's car, the yellow Pinto, and that she would drive Richard's car home for him. Lola was supposed to follow Virginia so that she could get Helen's car back home once they dropped Richard off.

McCain, the security guard, had picked up Richard's keys and wallet, which he had left on the counter of the car.

He handed them to Lola.

"You be careful now, ladies."

"We will. We will," my mother said.

Lola tossed the keys to my mother. Then Lola pocketed the wallet herself. Never gave it to my mother.

Lola followed behind my mother who was driving Richard's car, with Richard in the passenger seat, passed out.

They were on their way to one of his friend's houses. She couldn't take him home because he had a wife and kids. Richard was married.

Lola followed my mom for several miles until my mom drove through a yellow light and lost Lola behind her. There was a police man on the corner. Lola stopped at the light, so that she wouldn't run the red right after my mother.

The policeman became suspicious, something about Lola's behavior, followed her and ended up pulling Lola over. Lola was arrested for drinking while intoxicated. She had drugs on her. She was taken into custody and the Pinto was impounded. Lola ended up in jail for a week. My mother never knew what happened to Lola. Lola had no way of letting my mother know where she was or where the Pinto was.

That night was the last time Lola saw my mother.

The Pinto was towed to B&C Wrecking Yard. They searched the car and found a brown wallet with the identification of Richard Espinoza.

My mother drove Richard to his friend's house on Floral Avenue. Their names were Mickey and Dickey. They owned a gray and green truck. My mother and Richard stayed there until Richard could sober up some. After a while they left again.

Richard started sobering up slowly. He searched his pockets, looking for his wallet. When he couldn't find it he asked my mother where his wallet was. She said, she didn't know. He demanded that she tell him the truth. She denied knowing about his wallet. They began to fight. He called her names. She defended herself. Then he got enraged, grabbed a steel pipe lying in the back of the car and hit her on the head. She was unconscious and at first he thought she was dead.

There were many conflicting reports from here. Mickey and Dickey claimed to have been dancing with Virginia in the bar and that she was drunk. Richard claimed to have left her at the bar at midnight. A blue green truck was seen on Maplewood Drive, where my mother was later found.

An anonymous tip finally told the story like this:

Richard thought Virginia was dead. Cursing her, he drove her to the rock quarry in south west Albuquerque, off Maplewood Drive. On the way there she woke up and began to move. He dragged her out of the car, as she tried to fight him off. He took a screwdriver from his car and stabbed her in the back and the chest twenty six times. She was still alive. He took a pair of scissors and stabbed her more times in the lungs, in the arms, a total of thirty three wounds according to the autopsy. Then he left her to die.

She was found the next morning, having dragged herself two blocks, crawling on her belly, looking for help at the houses at the end of Maplewood Drive. A construction worker found her unconscious.

She was taken to Presbyterian Hospital and registered as Jane Doe.

Richard Espinoza did not go to work the next day. Instead he went to Helen's house, looking for Virginia. Then he went to my grandparents' house, claiming he was looking for my mother because he thought she had his wallet. My grandparents said nothing about where she was or that she was missing. He had eight or nine fresh scratches on his chest, and scratches on his face and arms and hands.

My mother lay unconscious in critical condition for two days. The Albuquerque Tribune printed a small article with the headline: "Stabbed Woman Identity Sought," on May 26th, 1975, two days after she had been so brutally attacked. The article said she was in critical condition and family should come and identify her.

The day the newspaper printed the article Richard Espinoza went to the hospital, claiming to be Virginia's brother. He did not have his driver's license, and said he had flown in from Denver and lost it on the plane. He tried to get access to the intensive care unit in this way and was turned away. Police detained him. They also detained his brother Jimmy Espinoza who had checked himself into the hospital for a bad back at the same time. They claimed it was a coincidence.

Richard Espinoza was told he would be arrested if he tried to enter her room again. Jimmy Espinoza was asked to open his bag and became belligerent when two bottles of wine were found in brown bags.

Later Richard Espinoza would succeed in getting himself into her room.

My mother lay in her room, dying, still unidentified, when Richard got himself inside. He was alone with her for a short time, alone in the room where she was clinging to life. He had hidden a heavy wrench in his clothing and struck my mother several times in the head, hoping to kill her off.

A nurse later noticed that there were fresh trauma wounds

Mi Vida Loca

on her skull, but nobody could figure out what it was from. It was so strange, so bizarre, so unlikely, so unexplainable, that no one looked into it. She died that same day.

That same day Richard's wallet was found in the Pinto at the wrecking yard.

In interviews with detectives, Richard Espinoza contradicted himself several times, regarding what he drank, what he smoked, when he left the bar, when he got home, how he got home, whether he took a cab, or walked, whether his wife gave him the fresh scratches on his chest or whether a fall from two small steps had given him the scratches in his arms and hands, and put the blood on his shoes. There were blood stains on the car, on the passenger door, on the front hood.

He refused to take a lie detector test.

There were two bloody rocks at the scene of the crime. They also found an empty can of Schlitz beer, his brand of beer. Winston cigarette butts. His brand of cigarettes.

In his car they took into evidence a white rag with blood on it, black gloves with stains, a chain with possible blood on it, a screwdriver, a putty knife, an empty can of Schlitz.

Later they returned these things at his request without question.

She wasn't important enough. She was a Latina. She was from the ghetto. There wasn't much interest in the police department. It took two days for someone to seek her identity. She was not a high priority.

Detective Rohlfs had pursued the case and was taken off and reassigned. Detective Rohlfs had tried his best, but he had no support from his department.

But the signs were all there.

His son put the case together, twenty two years later. And then it was too late. Too late for me.

After the Ayala loss, I spent my time grieving my mother's death all over again.

I had to face the horror of how alone she was, and how helpless I had been, even though I knew what happened. No one can explain that vision I had. I saw her chained to a truck screaming for help. They found a chain with blood on it in his car. I don't know what it means. I saw her. I know I saw her. People try to tell me it was a nightmare. I still believe I saw her. No one believed me then. No one called the police to report her missing. No one wanted to call the police, only because of the ghetto code, only because you didn't call police.

But what if my grandparents had listened to me? The police might have identified her sooner. My family could have been by her side. Richard could have never gotten into that hospital to be alone with her. She might have lived. She might have made it. She had been stabbed so many times, stabbed and bludgeoned. Stabbed with a screwdriver, hit in the skull with the bloody rocks. And still she had fought for life. Still she had crawled so far for help. She wanted to live. She wanted to come home. She wanted to come home to me. I know it deep in my heart.

She fought for me. And I fought for her. But when I tried to wake up my grandparents, my grandpa had thrown me across the room, told me to shut up and go back to sleep.

When I said I knew something was wrong the next day, and she hadn't come home, still no one believed me. I had tried, I had tried so hard, and had failed to save her.

I felt so responsible for her death. I felt I didn't deserve to live anymore, not after she died. I could never come to a close, because no one let me say good-bye. No one let me see her. I was the one trying to save her, and they kept me away. Now I knew how much she had needed me, and how much she had fought to be back with me.

There isn't a day I don't think about her. There isn't a day I don't miss her. There isn't a day I don't grieve and wish that I could be with her. I didn't know how to heal from the pain, even though I tried. I spent my life trying not to feel it. Now it was back and bigger than ever.

And worst of all, Richard was dead. It was like a cruel joke on me. I couldn't even close that chapter. There wasn't going to be revenge. There wasn't anything I could do. There's wasn't anything left.

After this point in my life, the darkness set in and never left me. I went through the motions of life. I had some good days, but I had died again with my mother, the second time, when I found out the truth of her death and her murderer.

This time I really didn't want to come back to the world. I went lower than I had ever been.

Only the constant and steady and vigilant love of my wife kept me alive, as it has so many times before.

26

I TRY TO KILL MYSELF A MONTH AFTER THE AYALA FIGHT, A MONTH AFTER LEARNING ABOUT MY MOTHER'S MURDERER.

I had stayed in my room for weeks. Barely ate, didn't sleep. Most of the time I just lay there, frozen, or I'd pace around the room over and over. I didn't want to see anyone, didn't want to talk to anyone. Teresa would knock on the door, try and talk to me, try everything she could, but she couldn't reach me. I was so deep down low and was going down lower fast. All I could think of was my mother. All I wanted was to die.

Then one day I get the idea that I have to do it. I have to leave this earth. I couldn't live with the pain, in this hell anymore. This thought was growing and growing and wouldn't let me go.

I always kept a gun in the house. I go down and get it and take it back to my room and sit down on the floor and put the barrel in my mouth.

Teresa is in the kitchen washing dishes. I can hear the sound of the water running and the dishes ringing. I remember that sound so well. I am thinking this will be the last sound on earth that I will hear. The simple every day sound of washing dishes. It makes me even more sad and I start crying. I hold the gun to my mouth and tears are streaming down my face.

Later Teresa said she had a strange feeling when she was washing dishes. She felt a chill, like someone walking over your grave. She comes to my room and finds me sitting on the floor, crying, with the gun in my mouth.

I barely see her. She stands there looking startled. I barely see her through my tears. All I can say is, "I'm sorry, baby. I'm sorry."

She talks to me, loud.

"No, Johnny. Take the gun out of your mouth right now. You owe me, Johnny. You owe me an explanation for this."

She's trying to scare me, snap me back.

I'm saying, "I can't take it anymore. I can't take this pain anymore."

She tries to come closer. I can feel my hand on the gun, my finger closing on the trigger.

She's saying, "Okay, calm down, Johnny, calm down. Everything's okay. Just calm down."

Slowly she comes closer to me. I pull my finger on the trigger of the gun, but she's close enough to reach me and she grabs my hand. I don't know what I'm doing. I push her away and then I hear the gun go off. It shoots into the wall. I can smell the smoke. Smoke is in the room.

Teresa falls back because she's been hit in the nose and the eye by my elbow. I look at her and cry more. Now I've hurt her. I'm not thinking anything right. I'm just in a tunnel of deep darkness. Hurting her just makes me want to die even more.

She says she's okay, she's okay. I try to get the gun but she grabs it and takes it from the room.

When she's gone all I can feel is pain.

I can't live anymore. I can't live.

I go to the kitchen. I hurry before she can get to me. I rip out the phone in the living room. I tear out the phone from the kitchen wall. I know where the kitchen knives are, and they are my only way to fulfilling my wish to die. I take the biggest knife I can. There is such a violent pain inside me, cutting myself with a knife doesn't feel as violent as it really is. All I see is blood. I'm thinking I'm going to be okay now. It's all okay now. Things are gonna be okay now.

I don't remember Teresa finding me. I don't remember her cries when she sees me in my blood. I don't remember her wrapping me in towels to stop the bleeding. I don't remember her going to the neighbors to the doctors when I was getting too weak to any more harm to myself. I don't remember our doctor coming and fixing me up.

I remember waking again, and feeling the same pain. Waking and realizing I was still on this earth. And all I feel is that I have failed.

Everyone's caring for me. Everyone's taking care of me, watching me closely.

Robert, Annie, Teresa, Ruth. All taking turns watching, no

one letting me out of their sight.

But all I have is this urgent feeling that I have to go. To go away forever. I feel like everyone is my enemy. They're keeping me from doing what I need to do. I need to go for good.

I know where our stash of medications is. I just wait. Patient. I wait.

There's a moment I am finally alone.

I go to the stash of drugs in our bathroom and take every sleeping pill I can find. I pour out bottle after bottle into my mouth like I'm thirsty.

Teresa finds me on the floor in my room. She calls our Dr. Voy in Las Vegas. He comes right away. Gets me to the Monte Vista Psychiatric Center. Keeps it discreet. Handles it well for us. They pump me empty again. They keep me sedated. Watch me. Suicide watch until I seem stable.

I get released.

Teresa packs me up right away to go to our training camp in Ruidoso. She thinks being away might do me good.

But once we get there I just feel worse. I can't come out of the darkness. This darkness has a hold on me, and I can't see nothing else.

But they've stopped me over and over. How can I leave? How can I end it? End this pain?

One night, I am in my room and I start banging my head against the wall, hard, hard, slamming it, over and over and over again. I can crack my head, I'm thinking. I can't last forever.

Teresa finds me, can't get me to stop. Nothing works.

Nothing she's saying I can hear. Nothing she tries stops the pain. All I can think is that this is what I need to do.

An ambulance comes. Police are there. They give me a choice. "Check yourself into a psychiatric hospital or go to jail."

I checked myself into the State Psychiatric Facility in Hobbs, New Mexico. They have me on a two week psychiatric hold. Suicide watch.

It slows things down, it numbs me enough, but it doesn't do any good. I just don't want to live.

After the hospital, I come out medicated, sedated.

I announce my semi-retirement right after the hospital. I can't completely retire because I have contracts and obligations and there's a lot of pressure on me to fulfill them. A lot of people want to help me fight again. But I need time to think.

In interviews I talk about my mother. About losing her. I also announce that now I want to find my father. I ask my grandparents to come to a press conference. I think that if someone sees them, they may remember who they are, who I am. My grandparents come. It's one of the few times my grandma is out in public, and with me. They know it's important to me and they want to help. It means a lot to me that they came. It means a lot that they care. I was in and out of the family so much, I am grateful to have them there with me. We feel like a family again. I have some hope.

I also always had hope that my father was alive. That he wasn't murdered like my mother had said. I had heard rumors

Mi Vida Loca

that he wasn't dead after all. That he was a musician. That he was an Italian. That she didn't know who he was. And even if he is dead, I still didn't know who he is. I still don't even know his name. My mother refused to talk about him. I'm hoping the media exposure will settle this mystery just like it gave me the answer about my mother.

But nothing comes. No answer.

I don't fight that rest of that year. It's the year that I am thirty two years old. I can't shake the depression. I just feel like I am doing my mother an injustice by living past her death. I'm on suicide watch several more times. I'm in and out of mental hospitals.

I just can't get up after falling down. I may have been undefeated for eleven years, I may have never been knocked down, but the fight to survive my own life has been the hardest fight I have had to fight, and I constantly feel like I'm losing.

Teresa makes me seek out help. Teresa takes me from one expert to another, from one hospital to another, from shrink to shrink.

I learn there are names for all my feelings. Now I know there is something called "survivor guilt." That surviving a loved one, feeling responsible for their death, can make you think you don't deserve to live. Something I have felt my whole life.

I also know many things I've done to myself are explained by letters in the alphabet. I am diagnosed with so many letters I can still hardly keep them straight. They call me ADD,

ADHD, PTSD, and BP. ADD and ADHD was obvious even from when I was a kid. I could never sit still. I was restless. Hyper. High strung. Loud. Running all the time. Wired. Crazy.

The Post Traumatic Stress Disorder explains lots of other things. Why I can't sleep. Why I am afraid of the dark and have to sleep with the lights on. Why I can't wear sandals on my feet. Why I am always ready to bolt, paranoid about everything. Why I have nightmares every night. Why I need to keep my back to the wall when I sit. Why I have to blockade my hotel room with a chair at night, just to feel safe. Why I patrol the house at night, every night, walking all around, checking every lock and bolt and window, making sure everything is okay, safe, secure.

But the bi-polar disorder is the biggest deal. They tell me these feelings of depression come from being manic depressive. The ups and downs, the huge energy I have and the low lows I feel. And how I can go between these feelings all the time. Back and forth. How I can be high on boxing and crash after a fight. They also explain the addictions are so strongly linked to bi-polar disorder. Almost everything I do wrong, they explain with the bi-polar disorder, all the compulsive behavior, ideas that I am invincible. Though I will still argue with you that I actually am invincible. Look at how many times I have died, and tried to die, and I'm still here. If anybody's invincible, it's gotta be me.

They give me medications. They make me try everything. It keeps things calmer, but I didn't feel like myself anymore. It's like I am gone. Checked out. In another room. I feel numb and strange, distant, weird, creepy.

I tell Teresa I don't want to take these drugs. If I'm going to be alive, I have to be myself, even if it feels bad. I need to feel like I am myself. What kind of life is it otherwise?

Then it's late in 1999. One day I wake up. My eyes are clear. My head is clear. Teresa looks at me that day and sees a change.

"Are you alright?"

I look at her. "Teresa. I want to fight again. I want to get back in the ring."

She studies my face. She knows I mean it.

She says, "If that's what you want. Okay."

A month later, in January of 2000, I won my fourth world title against Jorge Eliecer Julio in Albuquerque. Can you believe that? What a feeling that was.

It was a tough fight. He was a tough fighter but I did it, I worked my way through. I felt alive and I felt strong. I won the twelve round decision and you should have heard the arena. The fans welcomed me back with open arms, with so much love. There was a long standing ovation and I stood, with my arms raised to all the fans and I yelled out as loud as I could, "Albuquerque, I love you!" And Albuquerque gave me all the love back. It was incredible. It was incredible to be back in the ring and to win that title.

I could have been dead instead. But I was alive. Thanks to my wife who, like she has so many times, saved my life. I was back. I was strong. I felt like I was new.

And just to prove to you how good I was doing: late in

that same year our beautiful son, Lorenzo Lee Johnny Tapia, came into our lives. What a blessing that was, a little boy in our lives, and a blessing he still is. He's a cute little guy who looks a lot like me in miniature. A little ball of energy and sweetness. Loves his daddy and loves his mommy, too. Greets everybody he meets with the words, "Hello, friend." His innocence breaks my heart sometimes. I can see myself. I see how I must have been and I want to cry. And I want to protect him.

And I'll be honest. I want to spoil him rotten wherever I can. How can I not? I can give him all the things I never had. So, that's what I gotta do. That's all there is to it.

From suicide to fatherhood. It was a big year. And it just goes to show, something I want everybody to remember when they think of my life, you can always come back. No matter what has happened to you, no matter how low you sink, no matter how bad things look, you can get another chance, you can overcome, you can fight yourself back. There is love and hope if you let it happen. And there are second, third and fourth chances.

And I needed a couple more myself.

27

MY WIFE IS MY ANGEL, MY SAVIOR, MY GRACE, MY SALVATION. I have a tattoo of her name on my right shoulder. On my left shoulder is the name of my mother. The two angels on my shoulder, one on earth, one in heaven.

My angel on this earth is an incredible woman, and I'm not sure how I deserve such a jewel. Can you believe we're still married after all these years? I'm a prize fighter, but I think I'm no prize.

I am on this earth, alive, still able to fight, because of my wife and love, Teresa. I love her for her toughness and her softness. For her beauty and her strength. For her caring and her generous heart. And most of all for her intelligence. The woman reads four or five books a week. She knows everything about everything. She is the smartest person I know. That's the only way to describe her.

What she has gone through with me, and what she has been able to do for me, I will never be able to repay her for. That woman has the strength of a hundred others.

She became a mother and raised Lorenzo with love. I was happy for her to be a mom, because she is so loving, and she could give those feelings to her own child now.

It also gave her more to care for than just me all the time. It could get boring, I think, taking care of a big baby like me. I took a lot of her energy. And in the years after the Ayala loss, after the retirement, and the hospitals, and the doctors and the medications, I know she started getting tired.

I was fighting again and it felt right. I have always only felt right in the ring. It is the place of peace for me. It is the place where I am calm and in control. Where all my feelings are in my fists, not in my head. There is no place I feel better.

But even after I came out of the worst crash after the Ayala loss, I still experienced terrible depressions. I still hit such lows, that doing drugs was really the only way that I knew how to cope.

So the old ways were still the only way I knew how to deal with being me.

A woman needs to put her love to the child. I think Teresa allowed herself the room to be there for Lorenzo, and stop taking care of me all the time.

And I took the room for myself, to go back to the darkest thing in my life. My addiction. The addiction that I just couldn't shake.

I fought in the ring, I won in the ring, I lost my battle with drugs again.

I beat Javier Torres in Las Cruces, and then lost another controversial decision to Paulie Ayala. Like another loss could justify the first one. But what could I do? I didn't care anymore.

I went back with Don King again, fought Famosito Gomez in 2001, and beat Cesar Soto in Las Vegas, beat him on a TKO in three rounds.

I fought in London, where they have me an incredible standing ovation. For some people love me in Europe. I always have the best time there.

I beat Eduardo Alvarez in London, knocking him out in one round. And you're talking about an old man by now. I was thirty six and still had the knockout in me.

Teresa became the first woman, wife and manager, who took her fighter all the way to win four world titles, and I say she made the first one happen, too. My fifth world title fight was against Manuel Medina in Madison Square Garden. I won the IBF title. I was an old man already, but I wasn't finished. I'm still not finished. This year I will fight for my sixth.

Making it to Madison Square Garden was my dream, and it's every boxer's dream. All my heroes had fought there. Sugar Ray Leonard. Julio Cesar Chavez. Muhammad Ali. Joe Louis. Rocky Marciano. Sugar Ray Robinson. For years we tried to make it happen there. Now I had made it and I won a world title. It was a great moment.

I was still strong, still a strong fighter, but underneath there was so much trouble. It was as if things were never really right after the news about my mother and her murder. Things were better again, but I had fallen from my mountain, fallen so hard and bad into that low valley, and no matter what I had, what I had achieved, no matter who I loved, no matter how many times I climbed back up, I lost my footing

Mi Vida Loca

again, slid back down again. I just couldn't climb all the way back out of the low.

At this time, some of my family was coming back into my life. I wanted to see them, I had missed them. It had hurt when they weren't talking to me.

Now Raymond called and we were talking. He was out of jail, hanging with his younger brother, Bennie. He was in trouble again. Running from the law for attempted murder.

I saw Randall. He was staying at home now, couldn't work after injuring his back. Taking too many pain pills, fixing cars in his yard for a living. He has a daughter, Venissa, and she came to stay with us many times.

I saw Charlie, too. He was married to a nice lady named Elena, and he had taken his youngest brother, Frankie, in. But Frankie was bad. He was still the spoiled one, only he was a big teenager now, and Charlie was talking about how hard it was to deal with him. Frankie had once wanted me and Teresa to adopt him and we couldn't do it at the time. So I knew what it meant, what Charlie was doing for him. He was doing a lot for Frankie.

Then one week, I had taken Teresa and Lorenzo to Knott's Berry Farm and we were on the road back to Las Vegas, going back home, when we got the call. Charlie was dead.

Charlie had been murdered. Murdered by Frankie. Of all the tragedies in our family, this was the worst since my mother's murder. A brother kills a brother. It nearly tore everyone apart.

Frankie was seventeen. His mother Crucita had been in

prison for most of his life. He had shifted from house to house, troubled and rebellious, from Charlie's house to my grandparents' house. They kicked him out because one night he broke his curfew.

Then he was on the streets with nowhere to go. Annie went to get him, to take him to stay with me and Teresa, but Crucita let us know that she would press federal kidnapping charges if we took him in. We had to let him go. So he ends up back with Charlie.

Then one night, Charlie and Elena had gone out to a restaurant. When they came home they found Frankie sitting on the couch, smoking pot, getting high, breaking the rules. Elena was upset. Charlie started yelling.

"What did I tell you about doing drugs? You need to respect the rules of this house. I am raising you, and I am doing my best, but you need to listen! I told you there are no drugs in this house!"

They started to argue so loud and so violently that Elena got scared and went into the bedroom to call the police. When she came back into the living room, she found Frankie with Charlie. Charlie was on the floor, bleeding.

Frankie had gotten so enraged, he stabbed Charlie. Took a knife and plunged it to his body, to his heart.

Charlie was clinging to life. Frankie was crying, saying, "I'm sorry. I'm sorry." Then Frankie took off running.

Elena put Charlie in a car and drove him to the hospital. The ambulance met her on the way. They got him to the hospital, but Charlie had lost so much blood. He died that same morning.

Frankie was found by police hiding in a neighbor's dog house. He was held in a juvenile mental facility and tried as an adult.

Raymond was hurting that his brother was dead, and that his other brother was the murderer. He had tried to be so responsible for them all. But he had been in prison most of his life. Raymond mourned Charlie. Bennie mourned Frankie. Frankie had been closest to Bennie. It was crazy. A murder in the family. Everyone suffered.

I went to the funeral. I paid for everything. The funeral, the casket, the reception. I wanted to make sure the family didn't need to think about that as well. I got to hug my grandpa that day for the first time in years again. It was a sad occasion that brought us together.

And standing there, listening to the priest bury Charlie, all I could think was, "What's life for? What's the use of life? Why am I here? Everyone is always dying on me. Why am I still around?"

From that time I wanted to stay close to my family. I talked to Raymond all the time. He was on the run for aggravated battery. He didn't want to go back to jail. He had already served nine years for second-degree murder.

It was a sign. He needed me. I thought that's what I needed to do.

My depression had gotten deep again. Saving Raymond gave me something to do. I couldn't think straight anymore anyway. All I was feeling was all the pain, the regrets, all the old wounds, wanting it all to go away, wanting to medicate all the pain away.

I told my wife, "I have to go. I have to go away for a while. This is something I have to do. I have to get Raymond safe. I can't lose another brother."

I went and hid outside Kingman, Arizona. I bought a trailer that he could hide in. We stayed there together for a month, doing drugs every day, drinking, going insane.

I had a signed deal to fight Naseem Hamed. Then it was changed to Barrera. Teresa was inking deals, keeping up the front, keeping my career going without knowing where I was or when or if I was coming back.

For the Barrera fight, I came out of hiding and went on a press tour. I announced a charity fight. It was crazy. I was as deep into the drugs and trouble as I had ever been. But I'd come out and make it seem like it was all okay. Then I went into training in Big Bear and tore my left bicep. The fight against Barrerra was scheduled for November 2, 2002. It was two weeks away.

I fought Marco Antonio Barrera injured. It was one of the biggest fights of my career and I was so far gone from the drugs I didn't have any good judgment.

Everyone was saying, "Come on. Don't fight now. Put it off. Get your arm healthy."

My left is my career. My left is my power, my secret weapon, my strength. But I still believed I was invincible. I actually couldn't put my own robe on, needed help getting into my robe in the dressing room before the fight, that's how bad the injury was. But I thought I could overcome it. Stubborn.

Everyone in the fight saw I was injured since I'm known for my left and I never used it once in the fight. I lost the twelve round decision. For me it was my first legitimate loss.

The other losses to Ayala were and always will be controversial. But I did lose that day to Barrerra.

But the fans were with me. The fans gave me all the respect and all the love they ever have. The next day the papers wrote, "Barrera wins fight. Tapia wins fans."

A week later I disappeared again. I spent some time running with my brothers, running on the streets with family.

Teresa didn't know if I was dead or alive, again. It was too much. It was too long. When I saw her she looked at me, serious.

"Johnny. I can't do this anymore."

I knew she meant it.

But I also knew what I was capable of. And what I couldn't do. I couldn't change. I knew I was lost. As lost as I've ever been.

I said, "I've got a mistress and she won't let me go. I love you, baby. But I love the drugs more."

We separated. We separated without a fight, with tears, but with no bad feelings. We settled it all amicably. We talked about how to split what we had. How we would sell our houses. Split our responsibilities. And then I left. And I thought I was never coming back.

I went back to Kingman where Raymond was hiding with Bennie and Joseph with him. We thought it was all pretty romantic. Pretty cool. And the drugs didn't help things. We were high, twenty four seven.

After a month of abusing drugs, I called Teresa. I missed her. I was so low. The drugs were dragging me lower and lower. I needed money. I asked her to come and bring me some cash. She drove out from Las Vegas to see me.

She said, "You look like hell, Johnny. You look awful."

I was shaking. I hadn't eaten in a week. I had lost weight.

That night I had had a dream. In the dream I was shot by police and killed. I was convinced that I knew that I was going to die this very day in this very way. I told her about it.

She said, "Johnny, come home."

"I can't come home. I love you, baby. I'm sorry I put you through so much."

"You can come back. You can get clean."

"No. Today's the day I'm gonna die."

I was crying. She was crying.

"I'm not going to let you die," she said.

She was trying to drag me to the car.

I refused to go.

She looked heartbroken.

"Okay. If that's what I have to do, leave you here, that's what I have to do."

She got back in the car and drove back to Las Vegas. It was the saddest and most pathetic moment of my life. She had a parent teacher conference to go to. I had drugs to do.

She gave me my money and left.

That same day the Feds come and raid the trailer. A full stand-off with FBI. The media shows up. Helicopters circle.

Men with megaphones stand outside and try to make us give ourselves up.

The press calls Teresa. "How do you feel about your husband being in a stand off with FBI?"

She says, "What are you talking about?"

"Turn on your TV."

She called my number in the trailer.

"What's going on, Johnny?!"

I say, "I love you, but I'm not going down!"

The agents outside are calling out to us, "We don't want any bloodshed! Please turn yourselves in!"

I tell Teresa, "I'm not letting my brothers go down alone!"

Neighbors take Lorenzo in to keep him away from the media that has gathered at our house in Las Vegas. Teresa leaves right away to drive back to Arizona to come and get me. It was a one and a half hour drive from Las Vegas. She stayed on the phone with me the whole time she was driving.

Then it was suddenly over as quickly as it started. The agents yanked the door off the trailer and took everybody into custody. Nobody got hurt.

We had so much cocaine, the moment the door came off, I swallowed it all. Swallowed the bags whole. It was a crazy thing to do. But I never said I wasn't crazy. My crazy life has been crazy mainly because of me.

They booked me and Raymond and Joseph and Bennie. I was released and Teresa was there to take me home.

She drove me back to Las Vegas.

She took me inside. She fed me. I went to take a shower. I

came downstairs after showering.

Teresa was sitting downstairs in the living room with Robert and Annie and Ruth.

I was walking down the stairs and was already losing consciousness. I never told Teresa about the drugs I swallowed and I barely made it down those stairs. I can feel the drool running down my face. I am trying to talk, but I can't, and I am slipping away fast.

Teresa sees me coming and stands up, looking at me.

I can hear myself say, "Teresa..."

Then I fell back and things went black. That was the last thing I remember before the last time I died.

28

THEY SHOOK ME. They poured water on me. Ice. They tried everything to revive me but they couldn't wake me up. I was slipping into a coma.

Call 911. The ambulance. I was taken to the hospital. I was put on a respirator in critical condition. My heart was not beating on its own.

No one knew what had happened. It was thirty six and a half hours of hell for my wife and my family.

The media came down on that hospital like a swarm, helicopters circling in the sky, news vans parking all over outside. Everyone waiting to see what was gonna happen.

Jay Larkin, the head of boxing at Showtime, tells Earl Fash, our closest friend and supporter at Showtime, a man we always loved, to make up a tribute that they will air on Showtime in case I die. Earl says he cried the whole time he made it.

There were so many calls, so many well wishers, that the hospital had to install a dedicated line just for the people that were calling in to wish me well, to express their concerns and utter their prayers. They updated my condition with a new recording every hour.

Paulie Ayala called. Mike Tyson called. Obituaries and tributes were being written. Everybody was on a death watch.

Meanwhile I was on life support and Teresa was told that she was going to have to make the decision about whether to keep me alive artificially.

She told them I was a fighter. I was a survivor. She didn't ever want to talk about taking me off life support.

Thirty six long hours went by. It was like the world was circling around me and Teresa. Waiting.

Then, the moment came that I myself remember.

I opened my eyes. I saw the hospital lights above me, white and glaring and fuzzy lights. I tried to focus. Then I saw Teresa sitting in front of me, holding my hand. She looked like an angel. I thought maybe I was in heaven. Then things became clearer.

Teresa says, "Johnny? Can you hear me? Johnny, it's me."

Then tears came to my eyes. I was alive.

My voice is hoarse.

"I'm still here..."

I started crying.

"Why won't anybody let me go?"

I couldn't believe I had not been released. I was still in the world, still in my life, still in hell.

"Johnny, it's okay. You're okay now."

"I'm here. Why am I still here?"

"We're all here for you, Johnny. We've all been waiting. You're alive. Your family is here."

But I still cried. I couldn't help it. I thought I was finally free, but I was still on this earth.

"Why can't I go?"

Teresa holds my hand.

"There's a reason you're here. There's a little boy who loves his daddy. There are things for you to do. God doesn't want you to leave."

It took me a little while longer to understand what everyone else had been through and to look at my beautiful wife with all the love she deserves. I've died four times on her, and every time I wake up, it's her face I see. What can I say about a woman like that? She's my angel.

We cried together that day.

I told her I was sorry for what I had put her through.

She told me she loved me, but that she didn't want to watch me die again.

I promised her I wouldn't do this again.

We cried together.

I told her how sorry I was for what she's been through.

She said I can't watch you die anymore.

Then I ordered a Carl's Jr. hamburger. And I swear it was the best burger I ever had.

The doctors said it was a close call, and that I had pushed it to the edge this time. I knew in my heart that I'm not gonna get away with it again.

And I understood something else. I had not been released because God just didn't want me to go, no matter how hard I've tried to make him take me, no matter how hard I've prayed. God just has more things in store for me. And that's how I see it now. There's something left for me to do. A lot of things left for me to do. So I accept that fact. I'm here to do some work. And every day I ask for guidance, to make sure I know what to do.

Teresa and I stayed in a hotel for three days, just talking, thinking, making plans. I wanted to quit drugs. I knew they were ruining my life, my family's life. But I never felt it so seriously, that commitment. I really wanted to stop.

I finally saw the news myself, and the scenes at the hospital and the helicopters and the media, and I heard about all the fans writing in, and the calls, and the love everyone extended. And I felt, I owe it to everyone. I knew the drugs weren't working for me anymore. And they made life hard for everybody else. I knew I needed to get clean.

I went into rehab in Palm Springs, California. I stayed there for six weeks. And I got clean. I got clean for real, for the first time.

My sponsor, and my friend, the man who is like a father to me, Tom Crego, who I call "Pops," he was there right by my side. Right there, waiting for me, waiting for me to be ready, supporting me, talking with me ten times a day if that's what I needed, teaching me how to get through, one day at a time.

Tom had been in my life for some years already. He came up to me once during the worst time I was having, after the loss to Ayala, and my mother's murder stories, during the time I was spiraling down so bad.

He came up to introduce himself because Steven had

brought him to see me fight. Tom Crego was a boxing fan, but Steven also knew that he had 23 years of sobriety behind him. Steven had a feeling that Tom could do something for me. It was one of the nicest things someone from my family has done for me. It ended up being very important.

Something about Tom struck me right away. He's a huge guy, and he has this calm, this peace about him. He looked at me with a fatherly kind of love. I hugged him to greet him, and he hugged me back, but he held on to me close and spoke to me and said, "I am praying for you every day, Johnny. And I hope everything works out for you." And then he pressed something into my hand. It was his twenty-year sobriety coin that he had earned. He just gave it to me as a gift. That coin weighed heavy in my hand in that moment and I knew what it meant. I knew what he had just done for me.

I had always kept contact with him, even during the worst of those drug times. He was always patient. Never judged. Always supported. But now that I was really clean, he was there all the way, like it was meant to be all along.

Since I have gotten clean, he had taught me so much, things that I still use every day. He taught me that addiction is an every day struggle, that I can be clean and still act and feel like an addict, that I can make the decision every day, just for that day, not to use.

"Don't do it for today," he always told me.

He told me there would be ups and downs, but that I've gotta live life on its own terms. Not how I want it to be. Just how it is. Forgive. Move on. And that's what I've been trying to do.

I am the only boxer to come out of a coma and go back to fighting. Nine months after my coma, the time it takes to bring a new life into the world, I fought Carlos Contreras at Tingley Coliseum and won by unanimous decision.

And I can't tell you the feeling it was to be back in the ring. Back again.

The roar of the crowd seemed to never stop. Everyone was there. The mayor, the governor, all kinds of people from New Mexico. I said hello to the governor between punches.

"How'm I doing, Governor?"

I yelled to the crowd.

"I love you, Albuquerque!"

I soaked up the feeling, the fans, my life. It was amazing.

I have risen and fallen more times than a lot of civilizations. I have been down and out and come back so many times that I lost count. And every time I come back, the most incredible thing to me has been how much the fans have supported me, what wonderful people and friends I have in my life.

Lucky or unlucky, I sure have been blessed.

29

WHEN I CALL MY GRANDMA NOW, SHE HANGS UP THE PHONE. I say, "Wait, Grandma, before you hang up—let me tell you I love you!"

Then I hear the click.

I lost my mom, and I lost her love so early and so suddenly that I've spent my whole life looking for that love. Trying to find it again wherever I could. I wanted my family to love me, my grandma and grandpa. I've tried so hard to earn their love my whole life. And my whole life, I never got it right.

Still I try and tell them all the time, "I love you, Grandma and Grandpa."

My grandma used to smoke and I was always on her to quit. I used to take her cigarettes and always crush them in my hand. She'd have a cigarette smoldering somewhere in an ashtray, and if she didn't watch out, I'd take it and break it in half and tell her I did it for her own good, because it's not good for her. It used to drive her crazy. Cigarettes cost money. She was always mad. I always teased her with it anyway.

I used to bring her saints whenever I traveled and came home from a fight. Every saint in that house I brought to her.

I used to grab her if she was making tortillas and her hands were full of flour, and I'd make her dance, and twirl around the kitchen with me. She'd laugh even if she didn't want to.

Every fight I won, every interview I gave at the end, I looked into the camera and I said, "I love you, Grandma and Grandpa."

Now if my grandma is interviewed by the press, she says I am dead to them. I am not a Tapia. I am not part of the family.

We've had good communication off and on over the years, and right now, it's off again. And I'm praying that it will be on again someday. I pray for that.

I was always so close with all my family, but once I made it, everything changed. Everyone started calling me, wanting something. Everyone needed a car, needed a check for three thousand dollars. Needed a house paid off. Everyone taking money from me, and telling me they love me. Getting mad if they didn't get what they wanted, comparing what they got with what others got. Jealousy, resentment, anger. Sometimes these are sad things that come with fame.

I was the runt. I was the one who had to be put in his place. And then I made it big and left them all behind. So much conflict there.

In their eyes Teresa took over. They resented how much Teresa's family has become a part of my life. But Annie became like a mother to me. She is the woman who has always accepted and supported me unconditionally from the moment I met her. If I gave her a gift, my family was angry.

Robert G, Teresa's brother, is my very best friend in the ring, my corner man, the one man who has always been there, always been someone I could trust, loyal and supportive to the end, who has put his life aside so that we can finish my career together, together like we always have been. If I helped him out with his house or his kids or his car, my family was angry.

If I got a new wheelchair for Lala, there would be jealousy and talk.

I have always tried to keep things equal, but they never see it that way.

When I started calling Annie "Mom," they said I was betraying my mother's memory.

If I put Teresa first in my life, before my family, they said Teresa was trying to keep them from getting money from me. They called her a gold digger. They said she had a spell on me.

But there was once a time when my grandpa called Teresa "daughter." He used to hook his arm in hers and walk with her proud of her beauty. He used to drive all over town with her in his pick up truck and tell her stories. She used to go and buy them groceries, so Ester didn't have an empty house. She used to read their letters to them out loud because they barely read English and didn't understand. They used to tell her to leave me all the time, because I was no good for her.

But when my world revolved around a woman who has endured so much for me, and who has saved my life so many times, they said Teresa had a spell on me. They took her pic-

Mi Vida Loca

ture to a curandera to break the spell.

Now they talk to the press and say that I never come to see them anymore, that I have abandoned my family. They show pictures of me when I was a little boy and say I don't call or write or invite them to my house. That I have no love for them.

I gave my grandpa my championship ring. I call them all the time and they hang up. If I come to the house now, I am met with a shotgun.

My grandma finally talked to me on the phone one day.

"You think you're so high and mighty. You tell other people about us being poor. You wanna be in the limelight, go ahead. We don't care what you think. If that's what makes you feel good, go ahead."

In the background I can hear my grandpa. They've turned him against me, too. He's talking real loud.

"You tell him we're not afraid of nobody. Tell him I'm the master of my own life. I don't fear nobody. Tell him to come here and talk to me to my face."

I say, "No matter what you say or do, I'm still gonna love you."

"We don't want your love," my grandma says.

Now I bless them, I tell them I love them when I can, I pray for them. And I put it in the Good Lord's hands to take care of the rest.

My grandpa had a stroke some time ago and it shook me deeply. I wanna go over there and hug him and be there for him. I don't want something to happen to him and we are still apart. But I know there's nothing about that I can change. I can't control it. I do the best I can.

⁂

Everything changed after the coma. I still struggle with my demons. I'm not a perfect human being. But I've found a little more peace in my life every day.

I've also gone back to the ring and fought many more times. Won and lost and won again.

I had a fight scheduled with Frankie Archuleta in Las Vegas, New Mexico. But I got sick with double pneumonia. Was throwing up before the fight, but still went ahead and did it. Still I fought. Headstrong. Stubborn. That's me. I never learn. Later I had a rematch with Frankie, and I won it again.

Now I'm thirty eight. Planning for, training for my sixth world title. People may think I'm crazy for that, but I've done crazier things.

People say, how many times can you let yourself get hit. But it's like my grandpa said, I got a head so hard you can't hurt me. He pounded my head on the wall, and was proud later how all those beatings made me strong. Well, there's nothing left to hit. I broke my nose twenty plus times. It's barely in my face anymore.

No matter what, no matter how old, the thing is, I still got the fight in me. I still got a lot to fight for, a lot to overcome.

These days, as much time as I spend in the gym training, I also spend talking to people, talking to kids, going to the Boys and Girls Club of New Mexico, raising money, helping build houses and keeping programs alive for children everywhere.

I go to Victory Outreach and talk to reformed addicts and criminals, and we share our stories of overcoming and we share testaments to our faith.

I go to prisons and talk to inmates. I go to treatment centers and talk to people in rehab. I share my story as much as I can because I want to give others hope, I want to show how much you can overcome, no matter what happens to you in life.

And I give to the most important charity I know, and raise money as much as I can: the charities for women's shelters. For women who are in trouble, in danger, who are abused, who are alone, who are being mistreated, who have no one to turn to, who live scared, intimidated, controlled, women who are murdered if someone doesn't help them. There's nothing closer to my heart.

These days Teresa and I live together with a cautious kind of peace, a trust that is always being nurtured and rebuilt, and a love that endures all time.

We were recently blessed with Niccolai Thomas Johnny Lee Tapia. A new baby in our lives, a new life on this earth, a new little boy who needs us both. A blessing many times over.

She still won't put up with any crap from me. She still wonders what I'm doing if I come home late. She's still on to every one one of my tricks. And when I make a joke about the divorce we're finally gonna get, she still rolls her eyes in that way she does. And I still love her for it.

These days I understand more, listen more, appreciate more. I am a little less crazy, and a lot more aware of what it's all been like for her. And I try as best I can to make it up to her, to let her know how much I value her.

She still won't put up with any crap from me. She still wonders what I'm doing if I come home late. She's still on to every one one of my tricks. And when I make a joke about the divorce we're finally gonna get, she still rolls her eyes in that way she does. And I still love her for it.

So we take it one day at a time, together.

Some people believe in trees, some people believe in the mountains. And I know that all that was here long before us all. Some people believe you gotta cross your toes or who knows what else. There are many things to believe in, and that's all okay with me. But me, I gotta believe in God upstairs. He's never forsaken me. He's always there.

A lot of people have said, "Get over it. Move on."

And I've tried, Lord knows, I've tried it. Pops tells me all the time, the guilt I feel about being alive when my mom is not, that's the one that can drag me down. I gotta let it go. And I try to let it go every day.

I tried to get over it in the past. I've been on so many different kinds of medications, I've been to so many treatments and psychiatrists and therapy. It all hasn't worked. None of it. Not for the long run. The only thing that has worked, that's really, really worked, is giving my life to the Lord.

And that's why I'm still here today, looking at the mountains, hugging my sons, my two boys who need me now, who love me, and who I love so much.

I'm still here because God wants to show people that there is something out there for them, that if you have courage and you want to do something with your life, if you want to resurrect yourself, then you can go for it.

I've lived life to the fullest, and I've lived life from the highest mountain top to the lowest low of the valley. I've come back from tubes and hospitals and death and murder and madness. And if I can come back from all the crazy things I've been through, and if I can be forgiven and be given a new life, then you can, too.

You just gotta find your desire, your dedication to stay strong, and get what you want. Believe in yourself, and believe in God, and there's nothing you can't do.

Things are good now. I can't complain. I love my life today. I'm spoiled with hugs and kisses from my wife. I got two beautiful children.

There's a lot of things missing that I can't fix. But there's no use in getting high and getting myself numb, just because I can't fix those things. That's a fight I'm never gonna win.

I make a good life for my family. I love my wife, my angel, my baby, my princess, the love of my life. And to her I owe everything, every breath I take, every single day.

There is always so much to be grateful for.

There's always room for change.

I'm not perfect now. But I'm trying every single day.

I may fail and fail again. But I'm never going to stop trying.

I've struggled, come through all those hard knocks, and still I'm here talking about it to you today.

I've been in every kind of police car you could think of, but now, if I get pulled over, me and the policeman, we just chat and have a nice time. Things sure have changed.

I'm not going to lie. I miss my Mama. I still often wish God would take me back because I want to go see my Mama, I want to be with her again.

There are still days I just think about leaving this planet.

But God's got his plan, and you've gotta trust it. You can't do things your own way. You gotta do it his way.

So what's his plan for me? Right now he wants me to stay here and deal with my recovery. And that's what I'm doing, with lots of help. Help from my beautiful wife, Teresa, from Pops, from all the beautiful people in my life, all the great friends I have, my family, and all the fans who have never given up on me, and who I love so much, who have always prayed for me. I am so grateful for that.

I have people ask me, "Johnny, you made it through so much hard times. How can I do it like you?"

The answers are all right there, in every life of pain and suffering, they're all the same answers. And they start with you.

Turn in your guns, throw away the drugs, don't drown your life in the booze.

Love your wife always, treat her well, always.

Women are strong and intelligent and capable, but they are also our mothers and caretakers. We've got to protect them, support them. If you see a woman in trouble, if you think a woman is in danger, say something, do something, don't ignore the signs. Do it for them, for the children.

Treat your children with respect, always.

Don't beat your children, don't abuse them, because they are just little people growing into grownups who remember everything you do. When your kids are little they are helpless to what you do bad to them, when they are grown up they are helpless to all the feelings that are still trapped inside about the past. It makes for a lot of messed up people, people in pain, people who pass the misery on. You've got to stop it right where you are. It starts with you. It starts today, right now.

And I'm doing it all now with the help of God, the one who doesn't care if we're lucky or unlucky.

God loves us no matter who we are. So, I guess, it doesn't really matter if I'm lucky or not. I've got a folder of my criminal record that's two hundred pages long at home. I've given away as much as I've gotten.

God knows everything you do and everything you are. You don't have to do it alone.

He's the one who is always there, the one who takes care of us all.

I don't know what my future holds for me. I don't worry about it. I wake up every day and just try to be strong and try to do the right thing. Be the best that I can be. Lucky or not, that's what you've got to do, just your best.

So I'm telling you 'cause I know. Give up your anger, respect yourself, help others out, help those in need, find what you're good at, find your passion and go for it.

You never know when you're going to be called. You can die five times like me, or just once.

Yesterday's gone and tomorrow never comes. Live your life. Be happy. Do it for me.